desperate households

How to restore order and harmony to your life and home

desperate households

How to restore order and harmony to your life and home

kathy
PEEL

PICKET
FENCE
PRESS
A FAMILY MANAGER RESOURCE

An Imprint of Tyndale House Publishers, Inc.
Carol Stream, Illinois

Visit Tyndale's exciting Web site at www.tyndale.com

TYNDALE and Tyndale's quill logo are registered trademarks of Tyndale House Publishers, Inc.

Picket Fence Press and the Picket Fence Press logo are trademarks of Family Manager Network, Inc.

Desperate Households: How to Restore Order and Harmony to Your Life and Home

Designed by Erik Peterson

All Scripture quotations, unless otherwise indicated, are taken from the HOLY BIBLE, NEW INTERNATIONAL VERSION®. NIV®. Copyright © 1973, 1978, 1984 by International Bible Society. Used by permission of Zondervan. All rights reserved.

Scripture quotations marked KJV are taken from the *Holy Bible*, King James Version.

Scripture quotations marked NASB are taken from the *New American Standard Bible®*, Copyright © 1960, 1962, 1963, 1968, 1971, 1972, 1973, 1975, 1977, 1995 by The Lockman Foundation. Used by permission.

Library of Congress Cataloging-in-Publication Data

Peel, Kathy, date.
Desperate households : how to restore order and harmony to your life and home / Kathy Peel.
    p. cm.
ISBN-13: 978-1-4143-1618-5 (sc)
ISBN-10: 1-4143-1618-6 (sc)
1. Home economics. I. Title.
TX158.P34 2007
640—dc22   2007014780

Printed in the United States of America

13   12   11   10   09   08   07
7   6   5   4   3   2   1

*To the Family Manager Coaches across America
who have joined me in the important cause of building
strong families and happy, organized homes*

contents

> **You will soon break the bow if you keep it always stretched.**
>
> Phaedrus

> **The wise woman builds her house, but with her own hands the foolish one tears hers down.**
>
> Proverbs 14:1

> **There are risks and costs to a program of action, but they are far less than the long-range risks and costs of comfortable inaction.**
>
> John F. Kennedy

Is This Your Life?

Lauren M.
6:40 a.m. Monday

- The radio alarm blares in Lauren's ear after too few hours of rest.
- She jumps into the shower and speed-washes her hair.
- As she dries off, she stares blankly into her closet, wondering what to wear.
- She throws on her bathrobe. She'll figure it out after breakfast.
- She yells to make sure her three kids are up as she walks downstairs to get out the cereal and make lunches.
- Oh no, the milk is spoiled!
- She chides herself for not checking the expiration date and ransacks the freezer in search of bagels.
- Her twelve-year-old daughter storms into the kitchen and blows up because her jeans haven't been washed.
- Her eight-year-old daughter walks in crying because she lost her spelling book—again.
- As they frantically search room by room for the book, she discovers her five-year-old son happily playing a video game—still in his pajamas.
- She grits her teeth to avoid spewing angry words.
- She silently fumes over her husband's demanding job. He's never there when she needs him.
- With all the self-control she can muster, Lauren tells herself to take a few deep breaths and regroup so the kids won't miss the school bus.

- Never mind, she'll drive them to school and pick up breakfast on the way.
- No, she changes her mind . . . that won't work. She has a 9:00 meeting with an important client, and if she drives the kids, she won't make it.
- The clock's ticking.
- She's not dressed and her hair's still wet.
- She feels a migraine coming on.
- She wonders why this is so hard.
- She closes her eyes and thinks back to her college days.
- She graduated summa cum laude and was destined for success.
- Now she feels like a failure.

Nicole W.

5:30 p.m. Tuesday

- Nicole studies the list of tasks she scribbled before breakfast.
- She has been going nonstop all day and hasn't accomplished anything on the list.
- Her three-month-old is fussy.
- Dinner . . . hmmmm, she hasn't thought about that yet.
- Her husband walks in and asks what she's been doing all day. (She hates it when he does that.)
- The phone rings. Distractedly, she answers it.
- It's her neighbor calling to brag that she buffed her floors, cleaned her windows, and baked cupcakes for the soccer team. Dinner's in the oven, so she's heading out for a walk. Would Nicole like to join her?
- *No, I don't want to go for a walk with your sorry size-two self,* is all Nicole can think of saying.

- She bites her tongue and declines the invitation.
- Then she catches a reflection of her disheveled, out-of-shape body in the window.
- She's wearing the same sweats she put on the last three mornings.
- How could this be? This time last year she was cute, together, competent.
- She was thrilled to learn her pregnancy test was positive.
- Holding her baby for the first time, she knew going back to work would be tough.
- She resigned from her position to give motherhood and managing her home her full attention.
- Now her life feels out of control.
- She feels incompetent, depressed.
- She managed a team of people at the office. Why is managing one small person and her own life now so challenging?

Allison G.
3:17 a.m. Wednesday
- Allison turns over to block out her husband's snoring.
- Countless problems flood her mind.
- She thinks back to the day she noticed a For Sale sign in front of the house of her dreams.
- She'd always wanted a fixer-upper with charm.
- The location was perfect—a short commute for her husband and close to the school where she is a teacher and their children are students.
- They would enjoy working as a family, painting and updating on the weekends.
- The house was livable as is, even with the ugly bathrooms.

- The hideous kitchen wallpaper was the only thing she couldn't abide. It had to go immediately.
- She would look for a pattern that better expressed her personality—bright and cheery.
- Now, eight months after moving in, they've made minimal progress.
- Stacks of unopened boxes occupy most of the garage.
- Paper plates have become the norm.
- The bedrooms are barely functional. The kids have become accustomed to dressing out of the laundry basket.
- The bathrooms are still ugly.
- The insufferable kitchen wallpaper has yet to be replaced.
- She admits this may not be a bad thing—wallpaper reflecting her irritable personality would look worse.
- She blames her husband for the way things have turned out. He blames her.
- She doesn't like the person she has become.
- She's weary of living in chaos.
- She doesn't know how much longer she can take it.

Beth Ann J.
2:35 p.m. Thursday
- Beth Ann looks at her watch, wondering if her seven-year-old daughter is feeling better.
- This morning she complained of a scratchy throat.
- Now she wishes they had both stayed home, but she can't afford to miss another day of work.
- The fact that she's a single mom still seems surreal.
- When her husband asked for a divorce, she was shocked. She never suspected his affair.

- Child support has been spotty. She's stretching to make ends meet.
- She hates sending her daughter to after-school care.
- There's a mandatory staff meeting this afternoon, so her daughter will likely be the last one picked up.
- Then there's the question of dinner. Fast food *again*?
- She promised her daughter that she could invite some friends for a sleepover this weekend. Would she mind postponing—*again*?
- The house is a wreck. She hasn't cleaned in weeks. Dirty laundry is piled high.
- Her cell phone rings. It's the school nurse. Her daughter has a fever.
- Overwhelmed by her responsibilities, she struggles to hold back the tears and tells the nurse she's on her way.
- She should probably stop at the store for some food.
- As much as she deplores their unhealthy eating habits, she can't seem to find any time to cook.
- The bills need paying. They'll have to wait.
- She hasn't seen her friends in months.
- She blots tears from her eyes.
- She's got to pull herself together for her daughter.

Meredith B.
10:10 p.m. Friday
- The house is quiet.
- Meredith is home alone, clipping and organizing coupons in the family room.
- She turns on the news so she can catch tomorrow's weather forecast.
- If it's sunny she wants to power wash the windows.

- She'll persuade her husband to clean the gutters and weed the flower beds. He wants to go to the boat show, but that's not going to happen.
- She runs a tight ship. Never wastes time.
- Their house is spotless, hygienic.
- Their closets and drawers are fit for a king (or queen).
- Her children keep their rooms immaculate or risk indefinite grounding.
- She allows no food outside the kitchen.
- She constantly nags her husband to pick up his belongings.
- She never has time to relax and has no tolerance for family members who do.
- Her family doesn't appreciate the housework she does, but she reminds them of it often.
- Lately, she's noticed that her kids only want to hang out at their friends' homes.
- *That's okay,* she tells herself, *less mess for me to clean up.*
- Her husband is staying later at the office, even on Fridays.
- This morning she asked him what was so vital at work. He told her that the office is more pleasant than their home.
- He said he didn't care if the house is spotless. It's boring living with a woman who never has any fun.
- He said life's too short.
- Tonight she stays on task with her chores, but she's feeling lonely.
- She wonders if she could be driving her family away.

When Happily Ever After Isn't What You Expected

Desperation. Most of us arrive at this destination in one way or another at some point in life. We wake up one day and realize that things are out of control—and we're not quite sure how they got that way. Somehow issues about our home, marriage, kids, schedules, career, finances, appearance, in-laws, or blended families have collided, and life feels like it's on the verge of unraveling.

So where did things go wrong? Before marriage, all of us dreamed of a happy home. Hand in hand with the love of our life, we'd take on the world. We'd start a family and be exceptional parents. We'd create a warm and welcoming home, make family dinnertime an honored tradition, and host memorable celebrations for family and friends.

Sure, these were lofty dreams, but we all thought we could do it. None of us vowed to create a chaotic home and miserable life when we stood at the altar and said, "I do." But as one harried mother put it, "I love my family, but I sure didn't sign up for this."

Even homes that start out on solid footing slip out of control. Maybe you and your husband had good premarital counseling and began married life with a well-thought-through plan. Since you both had jobs in the marketplace, you split household chores down the middle—keeping your home neat, clean, and party-ready for the friends you love to entertain.

Fast-forward to now. Perhaps your first child was born a few months ago, and you had to return to your job to make ends meet. You snatch every spare minute when you're at home to rock your baby and pump breast milk. Clutter and dust have established strongholds in your once tidy adults-only environment. Now you wonder if you'll ever entertain—or even see your friends—again.

Or maybe you're the kind of woman whose feathers never have ruffled easily. Your parents and schoolteachers used to brag about your sense of calm and composure. Nowadays, just walking into your messy home at the end of a difficult day puts you over the edge. You stand there staring at the floors and countertops strewn with toys, papers, and dirty dishes. The kids pull at your shirttail asking what's for dinner, and all you want to do is walk back out the door, get in the car, and start driving. Anywhere.

Even the most composed of us can come unglued.

All mothers—even those seemingly perfect moms (which they are not)—have challenges and bad days. No one is exempt from a two-year-old's tantrums, a teen's rebellion, broken appliances, leaky roofs, faltering finances, cranky mates, and dashed dreams of a better or different life. There's simply no such thing as a perfect home, a perfect family, or a personal life without room for improvement.

However, there is such a thing as a *good* home—a place where family members (yourself included) walk through the door and think, *Boy, is it good to be here!* There's also such a thing as a good family—where uniquely gifted opposites live together in harmony and help one another develop their God-given potential. And there is such a thing as a constantly improving personal life—one in which you're learning daily to draw on God's unconditional love and promised strength to help you manage your home, balance your schedule, make wise decisions, love others patiently, face crises courageously, and grow toward your own personal best. In a nutshell, that's what you will learn how to do in this book.

It's Never Too Late for Things to Change

Perhaps you're thinking, *Easy for you to say, Kathy Peel. But I'm not like you, and you don't know how bad things are at my house.*

You're right. I probably don't know you and how bad things have gotten. But I do know this. Although I'm not much of a gambler, I'd bet money that I'm more like you than you think, and there were times my home was at least as bad—or even worse—than yours.

When people hear me introduced as America's Family Manager (after Oprah Winfrey called me this, the moniker stuck), they are sometimes surprised to hear that I'm not instinctively organized. After all, what's America's Family Manager, if not organized? The reality is that learning to manage my home and family did not come easily or quickly. Instead, it was born out of a series of failures. Some

"I will strengthen you and help you."
(Isaiah 41:10)

of the things you'll read are downright embarrassing for me to tell. You see, when I married, I was close to totally incompetent in almost every area of Family Management. These stories don't make me proud, but I share them with you to give you hope. I now can see how the lessons I learned from each blunder contributed to a system that today keeps our family and thousands of other families on track. Trust me, no matter how bad your circumstances seem now, they can get better!

Throughout this book, I tell stories about real families with real issues (including my own). The women profiled worked with me or a certified Family Manager Coach who has completed interactive and online training through our Family Manager University. These coaches evaluated the families' areas of concern, and together they created a plan to improve these women's household management skills. Throughout the book, you'll find details of their makeover plans, along with strategies you can implement to address your own frustrations in ten common areas.

Over the years, it has been an honor to participate in many household makeovers, some of them for television programs, others for magazine articles and newspaper stories. I believe that God put me in each family's life for a reason. Before each media opportunity, I always pray that He will give me the ability to focus on each family and their issues (not on the journalist or photographer who's following me around) and to know which solutions will bring them relief.

The people who open their homes to Family Manager makeover teams are not statistics or easy targets who want their fifteen minutes of fame. They are real men, women, and children searching for answers and hope that their lives will get better—and that maybe their stories can help other people in the process.

Homes can't be completely turned around in the time it takes to tape a five-minute segment or thirty-minute show, but people do begin to see how simple changes can transform their lives. Everyone, including me, learns lessons during the makeovers. We all want home to be a place where we can escape the stress of the outside world. We're all reminded that no one is good at everything and that there's hope for all.

During these makeovers, I've seen husbands and wives rekindle their relationships, single moms bring balance to their overburdened lives, and parents and children develop team spirit and learn to communicate in healthier ways. I've seen basements and closets once piled high with years of accumulated stuff become organized and useful places. Perhaps most rewarding, I've seen women rediscover their inestimable worth and find time for self-care and development. It's a privilege to see lives transformed when basic Family Management principles are applied. For me, nothing compares to watching desperation morph into purpose, accomplishment, and a deeper connection with family members. As you read about the women in this book, you'll discover how you, too, can make significant changes in your home and personal life—starting today!

"The best educated human is the one who understands most about the life in which he is placed."
—Helen Keller

But please note: The strategies in this book will not make your husband faultless, your children flawless, or your home spotless, nor will they make you richer or slimmer or solve all your problems overnight. They can, however, change your home, your family, and your life in many positive ways. They will make you wiser and more confident about how you spend your time, communicate with your family, manage your home, use your money, and care for your body. You will learn how to live each day to the fullest and get on track with God's purposes for your life. These are satisfying rewards for any of us.

What about you? Do you dream of a better life? Do you feel

desperate about a few areas of your life—or about your life as a whole? If so, you've come to the right place! And it might surprise you to learn that desperation is not such a bad place to be. In fact, it's a good place. Because if you're headstrong like I am, often you have to hit rock bottom before you're willing to grab onto a lifeline and get pulled out and pointed in the right direction—fast-forward—to a smoothly running home and a balanced, fulfilling life.

Grab on . . . it's going to be a great ride!

Kathy Peel

> **The woman who creates and sustains a home, and under whose hands children grow up to be strong and pure men and women, is a creator second only to God.**
> Helen Hunt Jackson

· ·

> **A home is a kingdom of its own in the midst of the world, a stronghold amid life's storms and stresses, a refuge, even a sanctuary.**
> Dietrich Bonhoeffer

· ·

> **I value this delicious home-feeling as one of the choicest gifts a parent can bestow.**
> Washington Irving

✳

CHAPTER 1

Thinking Rightly about the Role

What Family Management Is All About

When you feel desperate because some key areas of your household are out of control, all you may care about is finding that one magical tip or strategy that will restore order to your home—ASAP.

If that's how you feel, I have good news and bad news. The good news is that you *can* bring your household under control—and it may not take as long as you think. The bad news is that it won't come from discovering one foolproof technique. Instead, it will happen as you embrace your role as your family's manager and learn to use your expertise and creativity to direct the day-to-day functioning of your home. That's why I devote the first three chapters of this book to helping you understand your role, your unique giftedness, and your priorities. Please note that this is about *you*—not about making you manage your home and life a certain way. But I'm getting ahead of myself.

I must first stress that every home needs a Family Manager—a person who oversees the household from the perspective of an executive manager of the most important organization in the world. Family Management, like all other good management, is not about a dictator imposing arbitrary standards from on high. It's about sharing responsibility, helping each person find his or her niche, and empowering each one to succeed. In our family, I'm the Family Manager and my husband, Bill, is Chairman of the Board. We both participate in the operations of our home and take very seriously the job of building equity, if you will, into our home and family.

Like top-level corporate executives, Bill and I are peers and colleagues, and are committed to the same mission and values. But when push comes to shove, the buck has to stop somewhere—and the way we understand God's organizational hierarchy, it stops with Bill.

What! you gasp. *I thought you were an independent, opinionated, modern, liberated woman!*

Guilty as charged . . . and, quite frankly, it is indeed liberating to know that God holds my husband ultimately responsible for the Peel family. But I digress. The point here is that the job of Family Manager is a valuable, executive-level position, and we need to get over any preconceived Stepford-wife notions about what it means to oversee the goings-on of a home and family.

In the majority of homes, Mom is the Family Manager, but

in some households it makes more sense for Dad to be the Family Manager. I wrote this book from a woman's perspective and with women in mind, but the principles and strategies work no matter who the Family Manager is. And it's important for everyone in the family to understand the value of this role and treat the person who fills it with respect.

In some households, couples decide that, because of salary, benefits, job security, giftedness, and a host of other reasons, Dad should stay at home while Mom goes out to work. If this is the case at your house, keep in mind that both men and women deserve respect and appreciation for the work they do in the home.

Every Mom Is a Working Mom

Although we've made progress over the past ten years, the "Do you work?" question is still awkward for many women. Women who do not work outside the home often flinch at this question, because they work all day and their work is never done. Those who have tabled professional careers to raise a family find themselves not only defending their choice but also suffering unwanted pity: "How sad to think you gave up your career as an IT professional [or attorney, marine biologist, or whatever]." Others may ask them angrily, "How could you let your education go to waste?" People who ask questions like that have, in my opinion, never spent even one day with a curious three-year-old. Young children are not people upon whom education is wasted.

The "Do you work?" question can also be touchy for mothers who have jobs in the marketplace. They typically answer the question with what they do to earn a paycheck as a real estate broker, sales manager, nurse-practitioner, etc. Whether they spend twenty or sixty hours a week "on the job," they still have to come home and spend more hours cooking, cleaning, and doing laundry. In response to the "Do you work?" question, many of them reply, "I sure do work. I'm holding down two full-time jobs—one at my office and one at home."

"Whereas the service rendered the United States by the American mother is the greatest source of the country's strength and admiration; and Whereas we honor ourselves and the mothers of America when we do anything to give emphasis to the home; and Whereas the American mother is doing so much for good government and humanity, we declare that the second Sunday of May will henceforth be celebrated as Mother's Day."
—Presidential Proclamation, 1914

In 1969, the seminal days of the working-mother debate, I was a college sophomore. I first heard in one of my humanities classes that it was boorishly backward—at least in the minds of the campus intellectuals—for a woman to even consider marrying and starting a family rather than pursuing her degree career path. Almost forty years later, sparks still fly between people on both sides of the issue.

I read an article a few months ago that made me want to give the journalist a piece of my mind (which I can ill afford to lose). She stated that full-time motherhood is not good for women because they lose out professionally, not good for men because they don't get to spend as much time fathering their children, not good for the kids because they grow up gender biased, and not good for the community because women who stay at home with their children are not contributing to the broader community as doctors, lawyers, social workers, and such—which is their duty as good citizens.

I wondered, *What planet is this woman from?* I researched her background and learned that she teaches women's studies at a college and does not have children herself (at least at the time she wrote the article). I wrote a lengthy response to her article, but she did not respond. Following is the bulk of my reply.

When I became a mother over thirty years ago, I chose to stay home with my children, and it did not infringe on my husband's desire to be an involved father. He cleaned up baby vomit, drove carpools, coached teams, and to their delight and better health, cooked a whole lot of dinners.

As a stay-at-home mother, I did not lose out professionally, and our community did not suffer. When my children were young, I continued my education by reading books, taking classes, and learning new skills. I put in many hours volunteering at my children's schools, for community service organizations and political campaigns, and at church. Waiting awhile to pursue another career, in addition to my career as a Family Manager, did not compromise my ability to achieve success in the marketplace today as an author and CEO of a company. (I can't brag about my 401(k), but it's a small price to pay for great kids, a strong marriage, and a family that still functions as a team although we're separated by miles.)

When it comes to "women's work" and "men's work," full-time mothering did not cause my children to grow up gender biased. Our three boys learned that men are just as capable as women of mopping a floor and recognizing the aroma of a diaper that needs changing, and that women can run hospitals and corporations equally as well as men. Our sons also learned that smart management, of an office or a home, means delegating tasks according to age, schedule, and personal giftedness, not gender. And they learned that family is a team effort—a team made up of males and females.

Rearing children and managing a household are two of the most demanding and rewarding jobs. It is a great privilege and a huge responsibility with far-reaching ramifications for our communities, our country, and the world. What goes on in our homes affects who our children are today and will continue to influence them and their children when we're gone. As we spend time with our children—encouraging them at the breakfast table before school, listening to the happenings of their day in the car on the way to soccer practice, praying with them as we tuck them in at night—we are teaching them who they are and preparing them for who they will become. We are training them in how to treat other human beings and the planet we live on, how to determine right and wrong, and how they can contribute to making the world a better place. We're showing them how to express love and affection, anger and frustration, and how to settle conflicts. And most important, we're teaching them God's guidelines for living. This is valuable work—no matter how many other full- or part-time jobs you have, whether you're paid in sticky kisses or company stock—and it should not be taken lightly, for our children's sake and the world's.

Don't get me wrong. I am not advocating that every woman who works in the marketplace should quit her job and come home. My list of the best mothers I know includes a business owner, a physician, an interior designer, and a congresswoman, as well as women who have chosen Family Management as their only full-time career. All these women live balanced lives, and their families take priority over their careers.

I also know full-time mothers who don't take their job seriously. They fritter away time watching television, shopping, and running up credit card bills. Discontented and bored with their lives, they have low self-esteem and remain dissatisfied much of the time—not a good place to be, no matter what your job.

Here's the bottom line: Family Management is serious business. Bringing up children is not only a great privilege but also a responsibility that we need to take as seriously as career success, because home is where success really matters. Whether we're changing a diaper or closing a deal, our work has dignity, honor, and value.

The family is a great invention. When it's working at its best, the family unit is a uniquely loving and supportive place. It's where unconditional love finds rich expression and produces lasting rewards. However, whether we're office managers, Family Managers, or both, we are only human. We need help in balancing life's demands. We can't do everything by ourselves—and that's what family is about.

"The homeliest tasks get beautified if loving hands do them."
—Louisa May Alcott

Who Is Your Family's Manager?

When Bill and I married in 1971, we didn't have the options and opportunities of today's couples when it comes to premarital classes, counseling, and temperament assessments that identify potential relational rocky spots. You can bypass a lot of heartache by asking questions and discussing important differences and definitions before you say "I do." For example, how were disagreements settled in the home where you grew up? Did family members blow up or clam up? Who managed the household? What was your family's definition of clean? Did your family eat dinner together? How did your parents handle money? Who always did what around the house? How did you celebrate holidays? Did you open presents on Christmas Eve or Christmas morning? Most people consider how their family of origin did things as "normal." But if not discussed beforehand, when two views of normal meet on the business end of matrimony, trouble lurks just around the corner.

On our wedding day, Bill and I knew that we wanted to spend our lives together serving God and helping people—but we'd never discussed the nitty-gritty details of our homes. We had a rude awakening when Bill's normal and my normal collided.

Bill came from a family in which his mother did everything, and I mean *everything*, for him and his dad. Naturally, Bill's view of normal was a wife/mother who, in addition to her pastor's wife duties, prepared a "country breakfast" every morning; took care of all the cleaning, laundry, errands, and shopping; and prepared a home-cooked meal every night. I came from a family in which everything was done for me as well—but not by my mom. We had household help that took care of all the cleaning, laundry, and cooking.

Neither Bill nor I had any inclination or preconceived notions about doing housework. It had always been done for us. So naturally, Bill expected me to do it. And naturally, I had no intention of doing it—much less by myself. Talk about a culture clash!

But we were also products of the sixties—you know, civil rights, women's liberation, and equal footing for all. So it made sense to us to put aside our views of "normal" and come up with a new definition. We decided that I would be our family's manager, but we would begin our life together working as a team. Back then there were still plenty of traditionalists who wondered why in the world Bill should clean, cook, or do laundry since he was the husband. And when he became a father, they saw no need for him to learn how to change diapers or use a rectal thermometer. They thought that I, the wife and mother, would naturally assume most of the responsibilities for domestic chores and for the children in our young, growing family.

We came to the mutual conclusion that men are just as capable as women of mopping a floor and changing a diaper. We're in this together, we reasoned, and if that means crossing some invisible but deeply drawn gender lines that say a woman does this and a man does that—which back then it really did—well, so be it.

We also believed (as we still do) that if Mom is a full-time Family Manager, then Dad is more than somebody who signs the checks and doles out praise or punishment at the end of the day. Bill wanted to be just as involved with our home and our children's lives as I was. We were naive, though, especially before we had our first child. Neither of us had a clue just how demanding a new baby can be, especially in the middle of the night. Since Bill had to get up early in the morning to drive across town for an 8 a.m. grad school class and then head straight to his part-time job (which paid the rent), it didn't seem fair that he should take equal turns at sleepless nights. That was when we reassessed equality.

As our egalitarian arrangement has devolved and then evolved over the last thirty-six years, Bill and I have made changes based on what we want for our family and ourselves. Except for a brief part-time teach-

> "One's best asset is a sympathetic spouse."
> —Euripides

ing job and some entrepreneurial endeavors, during the first sixteen years of our marriage I chose to have only one full-time job as the Peel Family Manager—staying at home with our children and running our household. It made sense that I should bear most of the domestic responsibilities during the day since Bill had a full-time job outside the home. Then at night we shared the responsibilities—kids, dishes, baths, spelling words. As our boys grew and were able, they began to help out as well. We wanted them to grow up understanding that being part of a family is a privilege, as well as a responsibility. But it was more than making sure they had regular chores to learn about responsibility. We wanted them to feel the pride of "ownership" and the independence of being able to, in part and according to their age, take care of their things and themselves. We also wanted our kids to grow up understanding that it's okay for men and women to cross over traditional, invisible territorial boundaries. Nowhere that I know of is it written that Dad is the only one who understands finances and Mom is everyone's live-in maid.

About the time I began writing and traveling around the country to speak, Bill started writing and speaking too, so our arrangement changed again. We regularly studied our calendars to make sure one parent was at home while the other one traveled. We divvied up household tasks according to our new schedule, and although we are hard-core do-it-yourselfers, we outsourced more jobs so that when we were home we'd have more time for family fun. Someone else could clean the carpets at this time in our lives.

No matter what your stage of family life or how you manage operations in your home right now, beginning to look at yourself as a Family Manager can mean a fundamental and dramatic shift in the way you view your work and its importance. Consider the following core principles of good Family Management as you embrace your valuable role.

Core Principles of Family Management

- A household is an economic institution. Food preparation, child rearing, laundry services, housecleaning, transportation, care of the sick, the acquisition of goods and services (shopping), gardening and lawn care, home and car maintenance and repair, and financial accounting are all services typically produced in the home. Every home needs one individual who takes the leadership role for seeing that the home and all its operations run smoothly.

- Family Management is important work that millions of people do every day, whether or not they have another full-time or part-time job outside the home.

- The principles and strategies that successful business managers use will help the Family Manager create a smoothly running home. For example, just as in business, families need to know their mission and values, manage operations by department, practice delegation and team building, create standard operating procedures, do advance work, and build equity in relationships.

- Household tasks and responsibilities can be better managed when categorized into seven distinct departments and supervised accordingly:

    Home & Property—overseeing the maintenance and care

of all your tangible assets, including your belongings, your house and its surroundings, and your vehicles

Food—meeting the daily food and nutritional needs of your family

Family & Friends—fulfilling relational responsibilities as a parent and spouse, and with extended family, friends, and neighbors

Finances—managing the budget, paying bills, saving, investing, and giving to charitable organizations

Special Events—planning and coordinating occasions—birthdays, holidays, vacations, garage sales, family reunions, and celebrations—that fall outside your normal routine

Time & Scheduling—managing the family calendar and daily schedule; dispatching the right people to the right place at the right time with the right equipment

Self-Management—caring for your body; improving your mind; nurturing your spirit

In chapter 3, I'll show you how to set specific goals for each of these seven key areas—diminishing the potential for becoming desperate in each one.

• Family is God's idea, and He knows best how to make it work. By putting God first and seeking His wisdom, you will become who you need to be for yourself and those you love, and a better manager of your home, family, and personal life.

The Family Manager system helps people like you and me save time, money, and energy. It helps us get organized; carry on traditions; and create a warm, welcoming home. But there's something more significant, beyond the strategies. One of the main benefits of saving time is having more time to spend in meaningful ways with the people we

"To be happy at home is the ultimate result of all ambition, the end to which every enterprise and labour tends."
—*Samuel Johnson*

care about. We save money so we'll have it to spend on things like taking family trips, enhancing our lives, and giving to others. We save energy so we'll be awake to enjoy the finer moments of life—enjoying a night out with our spouse, reading a book to our child before bed, hosting friends for dinner. We become organized so we can reduce daily stress and enjoy the blessings of life. We carry on traditions that bond our generation with preceding and succeeding generations. We create a warm and welcoming home so that family members (including ourselves) and friends can enjoy a place of rest and refreshment from the stress-filled world.

It is vitally important to me to help my family (and myself) become all we were created to be. I want to bring out the best in them and have them bring out the best in me. I want this for you and your family too. When we rightly understand our role and take this job seriously, the quality of our homes improves.

The Family Manager Creed

I oversee the most important organization in the world

Where hundreds of decisions are made daily

Where property and resources are managed

Where health and nutritional needs are determined

Where finances and futures are discussed and debated

Where projects are planned and events are arranged

Where transportation and scheduling are critical

Where teambuilding is a priority

Where careers begin and end

I am a Family Manager

We are on the road to, as Samuel Johnson put it, "the ultimate result of all ambition." I'm so glad you've decided to join me on this journey!

Personal Reflection ✳

Managing a family is a huge responsibility and a highly important position for which no one is fully qualified. There are days when the job can seem overwhelming. To dwell on how we have failed or worry about how we might fail in the future is never productive. Instead, I've found that it helps immensely to approach our job with relaxed confidence and take our cues from the One who wrote the job description in the first place. Then we have nothing to fear. Being a Family Manager becomes an incredible privilege and one of the greatest blessings of life, a gift from the Creator.

> "God hath not given us the spirit of fear; but of power, and of love, and of a sound mind." (2 Timothy 1:7, KJV)

Ask God to give you courage, strength, love, and a sound mind to be the best Family Manager you can be.

> **Each mind has its own method.**
>
> Ralph Waldo Emerson

> **To be nobody but yourself in a world which is trying its best, night and day, to make you everybody else means to fight the hardest battle which any human being can fight; and never stop fighting.**
>
> e. e. cummings

> **You created my inmost being; you knit me together in my mother's womb. I praise you because I am fearfully and wonderfully made.**
>
> Psalm 139:13–14

※

CHAPTER 2

Your Personal Family Management Style

Learning to Work with How You're Wired

Success means different things to different people. For me, it means to excel, exceed hopes, and deliver more than promised. Just tell me what you expect, and I'll try to surpass those expectations. Freud would have had a heyday with my insecurities and need to please.

My drive to overachieve was not diminished in the least by the fact that I was domestically challenged when Bill and I married. I'll never forget the time, early in our marriage, when I brought a potluck dish to a Fourth of July church picnic— the kind where women bring prizewinning deviled eggs and blue-ribbon chicken salad. I brought one of the few recipes I knew how to prepare—a congealed fruit salad, which, not surprisingly in 100-degree Texas heat, turned into gelatin mush before the buffet began. I desperately wanted to grab my platter and ditch it in the lake when no one was looking. Instead,

I laughed it off and chalked it up to new-mother temporary insanity. Still, I worried because I didn't have the knack for homemaking other women seemed to instinctively have.

I remember the day when a prominent woman from church stopped by our house and there was no place for her to sit down because piles of laundry filled the living room sofa and chairs. The floor was strewn with toys. I was mortified because nice suburban church staff wives were supposed to keep tidy homes and be ready for drop-in parishioners. They were also expected to be scratch cooks and play "The Old Rugged Cross" from memory. I was way out of my league.

I wanted so badly to fit in, and I didn't want Bill to worry about what people might see when they dropped by our house. I didn't want my kids to have to hide under their desks when I brought cupcakes to a school party. I wanted to create a home where we could enjoy each other and the gifts of life, and make a difference in the world together.

Because I was so driven to succeed, I launched a one-woman crusade to become, if not the best Family Manager in Texas, then at least a candidate. I was blazing new frontiers, optimistic that anyone with a new college degree could learn to keep a home sparkling and running like clockwork. I mean, we're not talking about aerospace engineering here. (Although I decided later that training to be an air traffic controller would have proved helpful.)

To achieve this goal, I hit the books and read everything I

could find about how to clean, cook, maintain, and organize—faster, better, smarter, and neater. I also searched for a role model—a woman whose life I could emulate. Someone who excelled in the art of home management, who did things "just so." Whenever I found her, I was bound and determined to be just like her.

I wondered, though, how I would recognize my model mentor. Would she be wearing an apron? How many times a day did she vacuum? How often did she clean the oven? Did she alphabetize spices and canned goods? Could she make a bed with hospital corners? (The right question here, of course, is does anyone care, unless she's a nurse or in the military?) Could she see her reflection in her dinner plates? Could she operate a pressure cooker without summoning the fire department—or getting third-degree burns on her arms?

My strategy included joining study groups, attending home-based business parties, and networking with women in my area in hopes of finding a role model and mentor. One woman in particular caught my attention. Her home was perfect—de-

> "Effective management always means asking the right question."
> —Robert Heller

spite the fact that she had a two-year-old and an infant. Dinner was always ready at six o'clock. I quizzed her about how she ordered her day and how she went about certain tasks. She did laundry on Mondays, Wednesdays, and Fridays; scoured the bathrooms on Tuesdays and Fridays; and shopped for groceries on Wednesdays, armed with clipped and organized coupons. I tried to run my home the way she ran hers. I even cut my hair off because she had a short, no-nonsense hairstyle.

Despite my noblest efforts, I could never achieve her standards of housekeeping. I couldn't seem to stick to her cleaning schedule. I burned a lot of food. I turned a lot of whites pink and shrank Bill's favorite knit shirt in the dryer. I spent hours in front of the mirror trying to make my short hair work with a face shaped for longer hair. My self-esteem spiraled downward because I was failing to become like this perfect (or so I thought) homemaker. I don't like to fail.

Over the next few years I tried a different approach. Instead of looking for one woman to imitate, I observed and sought to learn from a number of women. I tried to copy the best housekeeping practices of each one. It seemed, though, that I was always taking two steps forward and three steps back. I decided that God must have designed some women to be really good at things like cleaning, cooking, and organizing. They instinctively know how to make things shine. They can whip up a gourmet meal in minutes. Their touch brings order to the messiest drawer.

I figured He must have made other women to be really good at other things, such as decorating, shopping for bargains, planning fun occasions, and nurturing relationships. Women like this will drop everything to walk their kids to the park or meet a friend for lunch. So what if the laundry's not finished—it can wait.

I struggled to understand which kind of woman I was. Then, finally, things started to come together for me. I realized that I had attempted to make myself into someone I wasn't. I had created a sort of alien being by trying to copy one woman's no-nonsense housecleaning schedule and combine it with another woman's ultracreative style of decorating and another's impromptu way of planning special events. They all modeled good ways of getting certain things done—at least for women wired like them. The problem was, I wasn't like them and before long, I—not to mention my home—was a glorious mess.

> "Always be a first-rate version of yourself, instead of a second-rate version of somebody else."
> —*Judy Garland*

Take it from me, you can waste a lot of energy comparing yourself to others and trying to be like someone you're not. You can spend a lot of sleepless hours berating yourself for not measuring up to other Family Managers and trying to run your home according to their operating styles and standards.

It's incredibly liberating to be released from the burden of trying to be someone you're not. This freedom comes from being comfortable with your own unique style of Family Management—and to do so you need to know where your current picture of a good Family Manager originated, and you need to know yourself.

How We Learn to Do What We Do

There are three ways most of us acquire our home and Family Management methods. Some women unconsciously absorb and accept their mother's management style. They grew up in a certain environment and learned to trust the way their mom did things as the way they should be done. Now that they're grown up, they feel pressured—by their mothers or themselves—to do things the same way she did, whether the style fits them or not.

I don't know the origin of this story, but it illustrates the way certain traditions are passed on to the next generation. For many years, a woman bought a ham for holiday dinners and sliced the end off before she cooked it. One day a neighbor asked her why she was throwing away a perfectly good end of the ham. She replied that her mother did it, so she assumed that was what you're supposed to do. The following day she called her mother and asked her why she cut off the end. She learned that her mother always cut it off because her roaster pan wasn't big enough.

Other women adopt someone else's style. They do something a certain way because their college roommate or favorite TV personality says it's the best way. Adoption can be a good way to bring new ideas into your life, as long as you consider your own strengths and weaknesses when deciding what to adopt.

Finally, some women have figured out how they are wired, and they value their personal uniqueness. They've learned how to maximize their strengths and buttress their weaknesses. They approach tasks according to their design.

Each of us has a unique way of doing things that

> "You cannot make a crab walk straight."
> —Aristophanes

fits who we are, and approaching life according to our design brings joy—and joy brings energy with it. Identifying your left- or right-brained dominance will shed light on your design and personal operating style.

If you are left-brained dominant, it is likely that you express yourself through order and organization. You probably like to make lists and handle details. You enjoy systems and routines, typically don't like messes, and put things back where you found them.

If you are more right-brained dominant, it is likely that you express yourself through creative means. You enjoy flexibility and spontaneity. You can tolerate some degree of disorder and like to keep things that you're working on in sight.

For the most part, organization and management theories have been dominated by left-brained thinkers, so most of us have learned left-brained methods of doing things, such as "Handle each piece of paper only once," "Finish one thing before you start another," and "Schedule certain tasks at certain times for certain success." This fits left-brainers, who like to carefully make plans, set their priorities, and schedule things precisely. However, this way of doing things overlooks a part of the mental process most right-brainers use. They think that people who make a big deal out of counting how many times they handle a piece of paper need their own help line. They like to juggle a number of different projects at a time and are okay living in a somewhat cluttered environment. This looks irresponsible and sloppy to left-brainers. But to a right-brainer, a loose grip on details makes perfect sense. Their "mess" works as visual organization and order. My sense of self-worth and perspective about life changed in numerous positive ways when I discovered and accepted my natural brain dominance and developed a personal Family Management style to fit.

Since I am right-brain dominant, I like to be flexible. If you tell me I have to clean house a certain day each week, I'll get bored. I enjoy change. I don't care what time we eat dinner, just so we all sit down at the same time and enjoy each other's company around a nicely set table. I like to work spontaneously. A spur-of-the-moment attic clean-out is more attractive to me than putting it on the calendar and dreading the time I've set to do it. I have no problem leaving dishes in the sink if there's something more compelling to do. I'm energized by challenging or unconventional situations. I keep a lot of sensory stimulation in my work areas—bright colors, music, artwork, photographs—and my desk looks messy to some people because I like to have my work within view.

My friend Pam is wired differently. She has household operation methods and schedules you could run the trains by. She gets pleasure from developing a procedure to tackle a task and then following that procedure until the task is complete. She would rather focus on

> "Respect . . . is appreciation of the separateness of the other person, of the ways in which he or she is unique."
>
> —Annie Gottlieb

one job, do it well, and do it thoroughly, than have many projects going at the same time. She likes step-by-step instructions when assembling or learning how to operate something new. She created an alphabetized spreadsheet for her family's DVD and book inventories, and if you open her pantry, you'll even find the cereals alphabetized—a good thing for houseguests like me who need to quickly find the Wheaties before an early-morning departure. When she needs something, she knows where to find it. Her desk is rarely in disarray, and I don't think I've ever seen dirty dishes sitting in her sink. Pam and I, though we're very different, are both good Family Managers. We just manage in different ways.

Understanding your right- or left-brained tendency will help you understand why you manage your family the way you do and why you get frustrated over some of the things you do. It can also help you discover more efficient and effective ways to get tasks accomplished that are compatible with who you are. Both right- and left-brain forces are equally valuable and

Don't try to recreate yourself. Figure out how to make your unique design and giftedness work best for you.

necessary in this world. What matters is that you learn to work and manage your family in sync with your God-given design.

Follow the Joy

Evaluation is important—and an important step in becoming a good Family Manager. Ask yourself the following questions and think about how God designed you.

1. What brings me energy?

There are some tasks that actually energize us. Sometimes I can work on a project for hours at a time—through meals and late into the night—and still feel invigorated. On the other hand, there are some activities that drain me—five minutes seems like five hours. There are certain things each of us likes to work with. Certain results we like to achieve. Certain ways we like to work—either alone or with people. Certain ways we like to be rewarded. Certain environments that keep us stimulated.

So, how can you discover your own unique style? One of the best ways is to follow the scent of joy in your life. I've found it helps immensely to make a list of the things you really love to do, things you feel you are good at and have a sense of satisfaction in doing. It may be planning an adventurous outing for the kids or hosting a dinner party for a group of friends. It might be taking up a cause at your child's school or mastering a computer program.

"My business is not to remake myself, but make the absolute best of what God made."

—Robert Browning

It might be balancing your checkbook to the penny or creating the best front yard in your neighborhood.

Knowing what energizes you will help you avoid activities that drain you and focus more of your time and energy on things you enjoy. For example, let's say your child's teacher calls and asks you to be in charge of organizing field games for the May Day celebration at your child's school. The problem is, you are not a detail person, and you hate to administrate, coordinate, or orchestrate anything. However, you come alive when you're painting or doing crafts, so you graciously answer that you cannot accept the position of field day organizer, but you would love to provide special personalized plastic cups for all the children in your child's class to use during Field Day and then take home as souvenirs.

Here's another example. Maybe each year you celebrate Thanksgiving with your sister and her family. You love to cook, and your sister hates to cook. But she loves to decorate the table and plan festive activities. In the past, when you've gone to your sister's house, the occasion was anything but dull. You played fun games, the kids won prizes, the decorations were fabulous, and the music was just right, but the meal left a lot to be desired—like antacids. At your house the meal was always gourmet, but the festivities were a flop. After learning your energizers and drainers, you suggest that you still alternate houses each year, but you would love to cover the cooking and your sister could take care of the decorating and activities. Everyone, including you, will have a happier holiday.

2. What patterns, themes, or elements do I see repeated in the things I love to do?

Look at each activity on your list and ask, "What is the best part of this activity?" "What do I love most about this?" Think about whom or what you are working with. Is it people, numbers, tools, words, ideas, techniques, colors, fabrics, food, or physical things? Can you identify any common elements running through your experiences? Think about what you are doing. Are you constructing, designing, cooking, creating, organizing, fixing, planning, or leading? What are you doing that is so invigorating? What do you think is most satisfying about each activity on your list?

"Before I formed you in the womb I knew you."
(Jeremiah 1:5)

Also think about the environment in which you do the activities on your list. Are people usually present and do they have a

What activities invigorate you?	What elements of this activity stimulate you?
Decorating my home	I love to get ideas from stores and magazines and figure out ways to do them myself for half the price.
Throwing a great party	Using things from around my house to decorate in different ways. For example, I used cowboy boots to make a fabulous center-piece for a Western party.

role, or are you usually alone when you do the things on your list? Does anyone admire your work, or do you just sit back and pat yourself on the back for a job well done? Is what you love usually easy or challenging? Is it most often familiar or different?

As you answer these questions and notice repeated patterns, you'll begin to see why you hate to clean up the kitchen by yourself but don't mind cleaning up when you have a team of people helping you. Or maybe you're like my friend who doesn't like help in the kitchen. She has an exact way she likes the kitchen to be cleaned, and she would rather do it herself so she can do it "right." My husband, Bill, loves teamwork and can go for hours at an unpleasant task if someone else is doing it with him. He bogs down in no time, sometimes even at things he likes, if no one's around. I am the opposite. I can get tons more accomplished if I'm by myself.

> The Family Manager system is not about turning you into someone you are not. It's about giving you sound principles and strategies through which you can apply your own personality and management style to achieve your family's priorities and goals.

For all of us, when we operate in the realm of our God-given capabilities, we will excel, be energized, and receive a great deal of satisfaction from what we do. On the other hand, when we're working at tasks for which we lack the necessary

skills and abilities, there is a predictable scenario of medioc-
rity and frustration.

Given a choice, we should always choose to mold our work
around our giftedness. Unfortunately, in the real world none
of us get to do what we love to do 100 percent of the time.
But knowing about God's design can at least help us be smart
about how we approach Family Management.

3. How can I maximize my strengths and delegate the jobs that drain me?

Realize that your night-
mare can be someone
else's dream. Is there
someone in your family
or network of friends who

"Too many people overvalue
what they're not and
undervalue what they are."
—Malcolm Forbes

loves to do what you hate to do? It's important to discover
what family members are good at, and put them to work in
that area. When they're working at something they're gifted
at, they'll usually work harder and faster, and gripe less—a big
plus in my mind.

For example, I have a good eye for style and color, and I
love to host people in our home. But I dislike cooking. This
being the case, I plan dinner parties when I know Bill can give
me a lot of support in the kitchen. I enjoy arranging fresh flow-
ers, setting the tables, and decorating the house according to

the season. He likes to cook, and I don't mind cleaning up the kitchen when he's head chef.

Our son Joel loves to organize things. We noticed this characteristic when he was young, so when it was time to do family chores, we delegated organizational tasks the rest of us didn't like—cleaning out the garage, organizing the pantry or videos—to him. This made everyone happy and gave him the satisfaction of knowing he was making a helpful contribution to our family.

Think for a minute about your circle of friends. Do any of them love to do what you hate to do? Maybe your closets are out of control because you don't like to organize, but you love to plan details and decorate for parties. Do you have a friend who is dreading planning a "sweet sixteen" party for her daughter but likes to make spaces neat and orderly? You help her plan and decorate for the party, and she helps you declutter and organize your closet. You both win.

Now make a list of the tasks you hate to do, tasks that drain your energy. What tasks do you lack skills or abilities for but feel compelled to accomplish? What tasks fall into the category of pure drudgery? You know, the kind where you experience no joy in the process, and the only thing you feel good about when they're finished is the fact that they're over. Are there distasteful jobs you could delegate to family members or barter with someone else who might enjoy doing them?

The fact is, great Family Management demands a set of

What activities drain you?	What could you change about the task to make it better fit your design?	Is there a person or service that could take this task off your plate, or at least help?
Paying bills	Put on favorite music, sit in a comfy place by a window, use a pretty pen, and have a reward ready for myself when I finish.	Sign up for automatic bill pay for accounts that offer the service. Reduce bill-paying time by setting up online bill paying at the bank.

skills that no one person has. There will always be jobs you hate. The trick is learning to work with your strengths and work around areas where you are not gifted and through people who are. You'll find some helpful ideas about how to do this in the makeover plans in the upcoming chapters.

Personal Reflection

I wish there were one easy formula for getting all Family Manager tasks done in less time with less stress, but no one way works for everyone. Give some thought to how God made you—your personality, brain dominance, motivated abilities, and personal style. Also think about your current life situation—the ages of your kids and their schedules, and the amount of time you can devote to keeping up with the house, shopping, and cooking each week. Being more aware of your personal internal and external context will enable you to make the most of your strengths and time.

Perhaps you're the type of mom who can't go to bed unless her house is in order for the next day—the kids' lunches are made, the kitchen is tidy, and you have a plan for tomorrow night's meal. Or maybe you're just not a planner. You spend the evening relaxing after a long day of working, playing with your kids, or both. And when tomorrow comes, you'd rather just wing it.

Whatever your style, consider how you might mesh your unique design with your Family Manager tasks to create a home that's a good place to be for all. If this sounds like an impossible assignment, ask God to show you how your specific gifts work with the tasks you have to accomplish every day. His help is only a prayer away.

> "I will lead the blind by ways they have not known, along unfamiliar paths I will guide them; I will turn the darkness into light before them and make the rough places smooth." (Isaiah 42:16)

> **Where could one settle more pleasantly than in one's house?**
> Cicero

> **If the environment [that people live in] is good, so be it. But if it is poor, so is the quality of life within it.**
> Ellen Swallow Richards

> **Cleanliness is not next to godliness. It isn't even in the same neighborhood. No one has ever gotten a religious experience out of removing burned-on cheese from the grill of the toaster oven.**
> Erma Bombeck

CHAPTER 3

Priorities Makeover

Making Home More Fun and Welcoming

If you met Karen, she'd probably be the last person you'd expect to have problems managing her home. When I walked into her house, I felt as if I'd stepped into a furniture store where everything is clean, crisp, and on display. You'd hardly suspect that three children (ages three, four, and six) lived in this home, with its meticulously manicured lawn, neat-as-a-pin rooms, and freshly vacuumed carpeting. Nothing cluttered the countertops. No child's artwork decorated the walls, and the refrigerator wasn't covered with reminders, school papers, and unsightly magnets. Toys were nowhere to be seen—and neither was fun.

But before I tell you more about Karen, I should first mention that families who have participated in Family Manager makeovers usually have a key problem that is the root cause of other problems. It might be that Mom can't seem to get the kids to school (or herself to work) on time. Or maybe clutter has multiplied like rabbits and taken over every room of the house. Perhaps a lot of money is draining out of the bank account each month with nothing to show for it. It's important to understand that good Family Management isn't just about creating order from chaos, running a household efficiently, or straightening out messy finances. While it's true that disorganization can zap happiness from families and quality from life, being overly organized and rigid can be worse. Some people just can't walk past a pile of clothes left carelessly on the floor, a dust-covered dresser, or a bed in need of making. Nothing is left for tomorrow. This was Karen's problem. Her home ran like a well-oiled machine. The problem was, it wasn't producing any fun.

Women like Karen can get so fixated on routines and orderliness that spontaneity ceases to exist, a death sentence for creativity and family fun. Children need spontaneity. In fact, they thrive on it. Their imaginations need room to roam. Homes that are not flexible enough to accommodate spontaneity can be stifling places.

> "You just have to learn not to care about the dust mites under the beds."
> —Margaret Mead

At Family Manager seminars I always make this statement: Kids won't grow up and remember if their home was always perfectly clean, but they *will* remember if Mom was a fun person. One time a woman in the audience raised her hand and said, "That's not quite true because

I *do* remember that our home was perfectly clean, and I also remember that my mother was not a fun person." Actually, she and I were verbalizing the same sentiment, and it's one we would all do well to keep at the forefront of our minds. Make no mistake: Your children will take memories with them when they leave home. The question is, how do you want your children to remember you and the atmosphere of your home?

Not too long ago, I was a guest on a national television program that focused on a family whose home management needed making over in a number of areas. The producer had cameras installed in their family room and kitchen so that what transpired between family members on ordinary days could be recorded. The family agreed to let the producer do this, but I thought to myself, *Wow, I don't know many people who would want everything recorded, because they might say some things or do some things they'd want to be edited out and not replayed.*

This experience serves as a good illustration and reminder that although most of us would probably never allow a television crew to record what's happening in our homes, our children's minds are much like video cameras, constantly recording what's going on around them. When it comes to how they feel about their home and family, we don't know which attitudes and actions will be edited out and which ones will be archived in their memory banks.

Although we cannot control everything that happens at home and how these events will affect our children, we can control our priorities—what we deem most important. I find that many parents have never taken the time to sit down and think about their priorities and the memories they want their children to take with them when they leave home. The fact is, our families will suffer if we don't take time to consider these things. If we fail to keep

> "We move through life in such a distracted way that we do not even take the time and rest to wonder if any of the things we think, say, or do are *worth* thinking, saying, or doing."
> —Henri J. M. Nouwen

clear priorities in mind, it's highly likely that the atmosphere in our homes will turn out very different than we dreamed it would be. Different in ways that everyone will regret.

While it may be hard to list your priorities when you're totally frustrated by a bulging calendar or growing clutter or your sense that keeping your home clean is a losing battle, stepping back to determine what you value most can give you a fresh perspective and renewed hope. To start the process of getting in touch with your priorities for your family, consider these steps.

1. Make a list of things that are most important to you. Your list might include spiritual growth, financial security, a fulfilling marriage, a loving relationship with your children, peace of mind, good friends, social status, a loving extended family, interesting work, travel, education, fun and

recreation, a great body, pretty clothes, a nice car, a beautiful home, a perfectly clean and organized home, or good health.

2. Answer this question: If you knew you had only a year to live, how would you spend your time, and what would you change about the way you run your home and life?

3. Write a paragraph describing how you want your children to remember you. List specific traits. If you're brave, let your children weigh in and tell you if what you wrote describes you, and if not, in what areas they would suggest you make changes.

Next, write a mission statement that reflects your Family Manager goals and priorities. In companies, a mission statement defines their goals and purpose. Long ago I decided that if the best companies have a mission statement, our family should too. After studying various business mission statements, I saw that they each addressed a certain list of questions. I adapted them and applied them to my family:

> "Perhaps it would be a good idea, fantastic as it sounds, to muffle every telephone, stop every motor, and halt all activity for an hour some day to give people a chance to ponder for a few minutes on what it is all about, why they are living and what they really want."
>
> —James Truslow Adams

- Why does our family exist?

- What are we trying to accomplish?

- What do we stand for; what is the heart and soul of our family, the beliefs upon which we make decisions and take actions?

- What is our basic approach to achieving our purpose?

- What is the overarching purpose I have as a Family Manager?

- What would I like my family to say about me when I'm gone?

- What is really important to me?

Here was my first draft:

To create a home my family would describe as a great place to be; a home where family members know they are valuable, where they feel loved for who they are as individuals, where they know they belong and can grow in their separate interests; a home that is comfortable and relaxed enough for those of us who can stand clutter, and orderly enough for those of us who like everything in its place.

After getting my first draft down on paper, I read in a business book that a mission statement should be no more than a single sentence and easy to remember. Following this advice, I wrote an abbreviated version:

To create a home full of love and comfort, order and flexibility, stimulation and relaxation.

As I thought about my mission for my home, I also thought about what I don't want my home to be: like a fast-food drive-through where family members rush in, grab a bite to eat and clean clothes, ask for money, exchange a few words, and rush out again. I also don't want a home where family members worry about making a snack for fear of messing up the kitchen and getting reprimanded or where they're always wondering if Mom will go ballistic if they don't have time to clean up their room one day. I knew that in large part it was up to me to set the atmosphere so this wouldn't happen. And while we don't always live up to my ideal, we hit the target more often than we miss it, because we're aiming at something.

A mission statement simply makes it easier to stay on track. It gives us an overall yardstick to measure the many decisions we make in a day or a week. For example, if cleanliness isn't a high priority in your mission statement, why are you spending twenty hours a week doing it? If intimate communication between family members is, then why aren't you working to find ways

If you aim at nothing, chances are you'll hit it.

to spend time together—maybe over regular family dinners or dates with your husband?

Knowing your mission and priorities won't make your home perfect, but it will help you make good decisions that affect the atmosphere of your home and the feeling about home among the people who live there. It will help you make wise choices about how to use your time and spend your money. You will have a map to help you chart the course, tell you when you are off course, and give you a point of reference to return to when you need to make midcourse corrections. It will help you know the best course of action when you have the option to remodel a bathroom or take a family vacation, when you have to decide whether to finish vacuuming or stop to play a board game with your four-year-old, and when you are weighing whether it's more important to finish the yard work or go on a picnic.

Karen's Story

As I mentioned earlier in the chapter, on the surface Karen's home seemed to run like a well-oiled machine. But here's what we uncovered upon closer inspection.

Every morning Karen got right down to work . . . cleaning the breakfast dishes, mopping the kitchen floor, and vacuuming the carpets, room by room—in perfect stripes, by the way. At the end of the day, the kids had put their little footprints all over the stripes, so she vacuumed again. Throughout the day she constantly picked up after the kids. She couldn't abide "messy" surroundings. She was so overwhelmed with housework she couldn't find any time to play with her children. While they played, she was working elsewhere in the house—folding laundry, cleaning the living room molding, polishing the silver, or alphabetizing her spices and canned goods. Karen never wasted time looking for ingredients, but her default priority—keep an immaculate house—robbed her of the time she could have been spending on more important things. Namely her children.

Mind you, I've seen a lot of out-of-control children in my day, and this certainly was not the case at Karen's home. As a matter of fact, her children were *too* under control. Karen had trained them to abide by one of her most important household rules—all toys must be cleaned up at precisely 4:30 p.m. This presented a problem for her six-year-old son, who loved to create art projects and build forts with her linens. But his projects gave her angst if he was still playing in the late afternoon, so everything had to be put away and in order before dinnertime at 6:00 sharp. If her husband, Richard, did not arrive home from work in time, he could find a plate of food in the microwave. Her rigid schedule ruled him as well.

On the weekends, it was more of the same. The couple worked in the yard, washed and waxed their cars, and touched up paint here and there around the house while the kids became masters at entertaining themselves.

Makeover Strategies for Priority-Based Living

PROBLEM

You're driven by your need to please your boss, make your mother happy, or ensure that your neighbors like you. Yes, you've got priorities—but they're making you miserable!

SOLUTION

Realize that we're all living by *priorities*. The question is, whose priorities are they? To live a satisfying life, your priorities must reflect *your* values and ways of doing things—not anyone else's. Use the questions on page 44 to determine what's most important to you.

PROBLEM

You want to establish goals and live by priorities, but you don't know where to start.

SOLUTION

Take some time to think through your priorities and establish guidelines for each of the seven departments (see pages 13–14). This exercise will enable you to see the big picture while providing benchmarks so you can evaluate where you are and keep improving and moving toward your goals.

PROBLEM

Your home is as sanitary and well-run as a hospital operating room—and just about as much fun. You spend all your time cleaning, cooking, and chauffeuring but never have time to enjoy your family.

SOLUTION

Spend a few minutes each week to plan some ways to create fun family memories. If you're married, schedule a weekly "upper-level staff meeting" for this purpose. Even on the busiest day you can set aside fifteen minutes to walk the dog or have a tickle war with your kids. Don't forget to plan for personal and couple time as well.

GOAL: *Keep a well-maintained home without forfeiting time for fun and building family memories.*

PROBLEM

You begin every day with good intentions to live by your goals and priorities, but interruptions and daily crises take your focus off your plan. After dealing with one issue after another all day long, you collapse into bed with the unsettling feeling that you're like a hamster on a wheel—always moving but never getting anywhere.

SOLUTION

Consider ways you could head off the next crisis by being prepared. For example, find a friend with whom you could exchange emergency babysitting services. Hide a box of toys you only get out to occupy a child when you need to handle an emergency. Having contingency plans will help you get back on course more quickly.

PROBLEM

A well-ordered home is very important to you. Yet your valiant attempt to get everything put away before dinner every day is stifling your kids' creativity and fun.

SOLUTION

Designate certain areas in your home where kids can spread out and work on longer-term projects.

PROBLEM

You want to have dinner around 6:30, but sometimes your husband doesn't get home until 7:30 or 8:00, so he ends up not eating with the family.

SOLUTION

Feed the kids a healthy snack to tide them over until you can all eat dinner together. Or feed the kids earlier and let them eat a light dessert at the table when Dad gets home.

Don't misunderstand. Karen loves her children, but without a clear set of priorities to interrupt her natural tendencies, she defaulted to the compulsive, left-brained side of her personality. Fortunately, when I began working with Karen, she had already recognized that their lives lacked balance. She sensed a void with her husband—their regimented lives left little time for them to talk or have any fun. And she was concerned about the memories her children would have as adults. Would they remember her as only a clean freak and not the fun mom she longed to be? Would they remember their dad as someone who came home and worked on the house like Mom did? Karen knew the answer all too well.

The good news was that both Karen and Richard desired to improve their family life—the most important first step because without desire, change won't happen. They both wanted to work on their marriage and add some fun to their family. For the good of their marriage and their children, they were willing to make some adjustments, some of which are covered in the chart on pages 48–49. If you've been running your home with a nagging sense that your family is not being well served, consider whether some of these solutions might work for you, too.

Karen caught on quickly, scheduling a fun break each morning when she and the kids would play cards or a board game. She tapped into her compulsive bent by actually putting this into her schedule. She kept the "4:30 rule," but she designated a special area in the family room for a card table where the kids could keep ongoing art projects and games out so they could be continued later without getting interrupted by cleanup time.

I encouraged Karen to think about and establish priorities for each Family Manager department. Here's what she decided.

Home & Property Department

I want . . .

- to keep our home clean and organized but relax my standards
- to remember that people are more important than a picture-perfect home
- to create a comfortable and welcoming environment
- to make our house user-friendly, as well as kid-friendly and fun

Food Department

I want . . .

- to eat dinner together as a family most nights
- to make mealtimes especially enjoyable times when we share laughter, tears, dreams, and ideas as a family
- to invite friends or neighbors to share meals with us often
- to eat breakfast as a family before school every morning

Time & Scheduling Department

I want . . .

- to stop spending so much time cleaning house
- to make decisions about how I spend my time by what's important to my family and me

- to balance work and rest
- to regulate our family's schedule so that we spend more time communicating and enjoying each other

Financial Department

I want . . .

- to spend our money according to what's most important to us
- to stop wasting money on things that don't matter to our family
- to teach our children a healthy respect for money
- to save money for a dream vacation

Family Members & Friends

I want . . .

- to always remember that relationships are the most important thing in life—that people are more important than a clean house
- to make dates with my husband a priority
- to enhance my parenting skills
- to learn to communicate in more effective ways with family members

Special Events

I want . . .

- to celebrate and capture special moments of our family life
- to put making positive memories high on our priority list when spending our time and resources

- to not be so overwhelmed with trying to make an occasion special that no one has any fun
- to go on weekend outings as a family as much as possible

Self-Management

I want . . .

- to carve out time every day to do something that refreshes me
- to schedule times for personal recreation and fun with friends
- to nourish my soul daily and grow in my faith
- to be purposeful about how I live my life

Perhaps you chuckle at the thought of having to deal with the "problem" of finding time for family fun because you are so adept at keeping your home in tip-top shape. Maybe you are so overwhelmed with trying—and failing—to keep your family fed and your house clean that you don't have much family fun either. That's even more reason to establish goals for each of the seven departments you oversee as Family Manager. In the next chapters, you'll find some tips on restoring order to these areas as well.

No matter what our situation, having our priorities in place is like using a 35-millimeter camera with automatic focus and built-in zoom lens. We don't lose photo ops because we're fooling around with the shutter speed and the f-stop on an older model. When we look at life through the lens of our priorities, everything is in clearer focus.

I urge you to take some time right now to think about your own priorities in each of the seven departments and write your own mission statement.

"The Best-Laid Plans (and Priorities) . . ."

No matter how precise your priorities and how strong your commitment to tackle each day's tasks with them in mind,

> "The true worth of a man is to be measured by the objects he pursues."
> —Marcus Aurelius

you won't get through many days without the unexpected happening. On days when life throws you a curveball, even a lot of curveballs, knowing what's most important to you will help you respond wisely. None of us can always control what happens to us, but we can choose how we react. Take, for instance, the day the dreaded stomach virus visits your home. Three children are whining in unison, and you have a choice: Get mad or frustrated, which will increase your stress level (not to mention your kids'). Or lean into the challenge, accepting a temporary cutback in family or work routines. That will mean using your energy to make the kids as comfortable as possible and cutting yourself some slack in other areas.

The point is that we all have choices. Part of responding to the unexpected is learning to see situations for what they are, not for what we imagine them to be. It's easy to blow things out of proportion, needlessly raising our stress level.

Let's say your dog is vomiting on the carpet, your ten-year-old has decided to cook dinner and just dropped a jar of spaghetti sauce on the tile floor, your five-year-old and your seven-year-old are starting World War III in the backyard, and your husband calls to say he's bringing a friend home for dinner. You have some choices: You could beat the dog, tell your daughter that only a stupid person would pick up a jar of sauce with wet hands, knock your boys' heads together to teach them that violence isn't a way to solve problems, and tell your husband that you're not running a restaurant.

Or you could stop and ask God for patience, wisdom, and the ability to remain calm and not say anything you'll regret later. Then you could tell your daughter you'll help her clean up the broken glass in a few minutes. You put the dog in the backyard with the boys, telling them to take care of her, thereby distracting their attention from the fight. While cleaning up the dog mess, you call your husband and ask him to take the long way home, buying yourself time to clean up the kitchen and pull something out of the freezer for dinner.

The point is that we do ourselves and our families a favor when we're anchored by our priorities and are able to wisely and calmly meet the inevitable crises we face day in and day out. That is easier when we bend with the interruptions instead of standing against them.

Facing the unexpected wisely also means sometimes taking the long view when deciding what's most important at any given moment. Your investment in comforting your discouraged daughter will pay far higher dividends than a vacuumed house. Attending your son's basketball game in another city as a family speaks volumes to him about his worth. And making a snowman together might do more for family morale than a day spent wielding dust rags and cleaning musty closets.

Here's the bottom line: The choices we make day in and day out involve a lot more than how often we vacuum, when we clean house, and how we organize our closets. Home isn't just a place to hang a hat; it's a place to restore souls, find shelter from outside pressures, grow support for talents, and receive inspiration, comfort, and aid. It is a place where family members learn to love and be loved.

Personal Reflection

Good Family Management is about a lot more than providing a clean house and an orderly environment. It's about nurturing our families and helping them connect in meaningful ways with each other, with the outside world, and perhaps most important, with their own talents, skills, and spirits so they become the people God created them to be. It's about creating an atmosphere in which our families can enjoy living, laughing, and learning together.

"A cheerful heart is good medicine." (Proverbs 17:22)

What's the fun quotient at your home? Research has shown that joyful laughter causes the brain to create endorphins that relieve stress and activate the immune system. Our families—as well as ourselves—need a dose of this kind of medicine on a regular basis.

If your family ranked your home on a scale of zero to five, zero being unpleasant and not fun and five being pleasant and fun, what do you think your score would be?

> **There is no more lovely, friendly, and charming relationship, communion, or company than a good marriage.**
>
> Martin Luther

....

> **Keep your eyes wide open before marriage, half shut afterwards.**
>
> Benjamin Franklin

....

> **One who looks for a friend without faults will have none.**
>
> Hasidic saying

CHAPTER 4

Marriage Communication Makeover

Getting Back on the Road to Happily Ever After

Bill and I recently celebrated our thirty-sixth anniversary. Truth be known, we've been happily married for about thirty years. There are just some years we wish we could do over. On our wedding day we promised that we would not divorce, but we didn't promise not to murder—and there are times when we'd like to wring each other's neck. Of course, I'm teasing (sort of).

Joking aside, marriage is one of the greatest blessings of our lives. It's wonderful to have someone greet you with a hug after a hard day; share your dreams, joys, tears, and fears; believe that you're still beautiful or handsome as youth fades; care for you tenderly when you're ill; and remind you of God's love and their love when the world treats you harshly.

Marriage also takes a lot of hard work. It is difficult (sometimes painfully so) to learn to forgive when you're deeply hurt, defer to what your mate prefers, overlook the hundredth time he forgot to take out the trash, own up to what you did wrong, endure criticism without lashing back, and live with unmet expectations. But every ounce of work you put into your marriage is worth it.

Every week in every state, couples begin divorce proceedings. Yet there's probably not a couple in the world who entered marriage thinking, *No way will this marriage work. Our goal is to make each other miserable.* In many cases, the invisible wall that now separates them was erected over time by little frustrations that grew into big issues that might have been avoided.

Perhaps that describes your previous marriage, and you are now raising your kids alone. As a single parent, you face the same struggles as other Family Managers, and on top of that, you don't have the support of a spouse to share the workload and the emotional responsibilities at home. Although this chapter is geared toward those who are married, I think you'll find that some of the principles will be applicable for you and your relationships.

Over the years, I've worked with a number of couples whose marriages were degenerating. Although every situation is unique and multifaceted, some simple, basic issues surface between almost every troubled couple.

The following stories of two all-American families illustrate a problem that plagues many. Both of these marriages were heading for the rocks. I worked with each couple, suggesting practical solutions to relieve relational tension, foster healthy communication, and create a more pleasant atmosphere in their home. I'll share that part of the story with you in a moment. But first I want you to read these short overviews and see if you can identify the problem both husbands had in common.

Bonnie's Story

Before Bonnie married Dan and became the mother of three children within four years, she managed one hundred volunteers at a community service agency. She had dreamed that she would manage a calm, happy home—the kind of home her children would be eager to share with their friends. Like so many moms, she was frustrated that her dreams and her reality were so far apart.

> "The mind is its own place, and in itself can make a heaven of hell, a hell of heaven."
> —John Milton

Despite the fact that she got up early and hardly stopped to breathe until she fell into bed at night exhausted, their home was very, very messy. The kitchen countertops were covered with dishes, mail, and craft supplies. Baby equipment and toys dominated the family room. Mounds of dirty clothes and sundry items needing to be put in storage covered the utility room floor. Chaos and clutter reigned in other rooms as well.

Dan, too, was frustrated. His dream home included a place for everything with everything in its place. He had trouble understanding why this wasn't the case in their home. After all, Bonnie used to manage a big office. He was puzzled as to why a pile of unfolded laundry always seemed to fill his favorite family room chair. His job was stressful, and he resented coming home every day to mess and more stress. He wondered what in the world Bonnie did all day, which infuriated her. Their relationship was rapidly deteriorating.

Tracy's Story

Tracy and John, along with their three young children, had moved into a new home two years ago. Tracy adored her home, but she was frustrated on a number of fronts. First and foremost were the toys—a lot of toys—in literally every room. Tracy had all but given up trying to corral and organize all the toys, many of which had a jillion pieces, and by default they had free rein of the floors and furniture. It irritated John to come home and have to move toys in order to sit down and relax. It irritated Tracy that this irritated John.

Their basement was also problematic. It was filled to the brim with random items and unpacked boxes from their move. This had become a sore spot in their marriage, infecting their relationship in other ways too. John wanted to set up an office in the basement so he could do some of his work from home. He couldn't understand why Tracy couldn't find the time to clear an area so he could do this. After all, he reasoned, he was spending twelve hours a day, five days a week, working to support their family and pay the mortgage on their nice new house. He resented her inability to block out a day or two to do this one thing for him. She resented the fact that he had made this an issue. Their relationship was deteriorating too.

If you think neither one of these guys had a clue as to what it takes to manage a home and family, you're right. But whose fault was that? I remember when this issue hit home with me.

Bill and Kathy's Not-So-Excellent Adventure

Vacation is a word that should conjure up memories of relaxation, refreshment, and fun times as a family. For years, the word meant frustration for me.

It never failed. The day we headed out the driveway for our summer trip to Colorado, I was in a bad mood. Here's why. For weeks prior to our departure I had been busy making reservations; charting our route; getting the car serviced; and making arrangements for the dogs, the plants, the mail, the yard, and the newspaper. I'd also gathered and packed all the paraphernalia needed to feed, dress, and occupy three boys en route and after we arrived. I created travel games, prepared picnic lunches, and worked up some serious resentment. I seethed because Bill seemed to be oblivious to all my toil. He would just pack his own suitcase, load his fishing gear, and be raring to go.

I smoldered most of the way to Colorado, whining that I was exhausted, complaining that I never got a vacation, griping that all he did was "show up." By the time we hit the Continental Divide, we, too, were divided. We'd turn up the audio book in the backseat so the kids couldn't hear our angry words. By the time we reached our destination, we were emotionally spent and ready to call a truce. We had missed some beautiful scenery and sixteen hours brimming with opportunity to make fun memories with the kids—largely due to poor management on my part.

You heard me right. I regret my behavior, and I'll take the lion's share of the blame. Why? Because I expected Bill to read my mind, know exactly what to do, and take the initiative to help prepare for our vacation. And in all honesty, he did do some things to help. But in my mind, it was a token effort. Instead of making him feel like my partner in the advance work for our trip, I wallowed in self-pity and resentment.

Bonnie, Tracy, and I all needed to take a lesson from business managers. If we want to be successful managers, we need to do some internal marketing: educate team members, communicate with them in positive ways, and help them succeed at their jobs.

> "Marriage is not just spiritual communion and passionate embraces; marriage is also three meals a day, sharing the workload and remembering to carry out the trash."
>
> —Dr. Joyce Brothers

Educating Your Spouse

Think about it. If you went to your husband's office and wanted to help him out, would you know what to do? Would you understand his time limitations and deadlines? when and how he interfaced with coworkers and clients? where to find the tools needed to complete a task? Probably not. Neither do most men understand what it takes to keep home and family operations running smoothly. Granted, men have a propensity to compartmentalize their lives, while we women tend to grasp the big picture more easily and quickly recognize what needs to be done. Our husbands' focus on one thing at a time often keeps them from noticing

"It's no good saying you can't afford to look after your staff. You can't afford not to. Treating your staff better will make your business perform better. It's that simple."
—Tom Peters

all the things that we see that need to be done. Don't jump to the conclusion that your husband is a selfish oaf before you take time to help him see what running a household entails.

I suggest that you choose a time when dinner's not burning, the kids aren't arguing, the roof's not leaking, and you feel emotionally stable—surely there are a few days of the month when this is true—to talk with your husband sincerely, and without blaming, about your job description as your family's manager. Keep in mind that reason, not emotion, catches

Who's Responsible for What

Home & Property
- Picking up clutter
- Cleaning the kitchen
- Cleaning bathrooms
- Cleaning the family room
- Sweeping/mopping/waxing floors
- Dusting
- Vacuuming
- Making beds
- Changing sheets
- Doing laundry
- Taking clothes to dry cleaner
- Mending
- Shopping for clothing and accessories
- Shopping for household items
- Organizing closets and drawers
- Organizing garage, attic, basement
- Collecting and taking out trash
- Recycling
- Performing household repairs and maintenance
- Contacting repair services
- Decorating
- Yard work
- Maintaining outdoor furniture and equipment
- Car maintenance
- Watering plants
- Cleaning carpets
- Washing windows

Food & Meals
- Meal planning
- Creating a grocery list
- Shopping for groceries
- Making breakfast
- Making lunches
- Cooking dinner
- Cleaning up after meals
- Planning and orchestrating dinner parties
- Keeping up with coupons
- Feeding the baby or young children
- Organizing the pantry
- Planning and taking food to special functions

Family & Friends
- Caring for small children
- Arranging for child care
- Dropping off/picking up/arranging transportation for school
- Bathing the kids
- Reading to the kids
- Putting the kids to bed
- Researching and registering kids for activities
- Transporting kids to music lessons, athletic practices, etc.
- Participating in school and other events with children
- Helping with homework
- Purchasing school supplies
- Teaching kids right and wrong
- Disciplining kids
- Planning creative activities for kids
- Monitoring television, music, and the Internet
- Scheduling playdates
- Teaching manners and social skills
- Taking kids to the doctor and dentist
- Overseeing college testing/application process

- Traveling to visit potential colleges
- Arranging family outings
- Arranging date nights with spouse
- Caring for aging parents and in-laws
- Keeping up with extended family
- Buying presents for relatives and friends
- Sending greeting cards
- Writing thank-you notes
- Caring for pets
- Overseeing relationships with neighbors

Money & Finances
- Organizing bills
- Paying bills
- Balancing checkbook
- Selecting appropriate investments
- Establishing credit
- Creating a budget
- Researching and buying insurance
- Working with attorney to create/update will
- Creating saving plans for big things like college
- Shopping for best deals
- Filing health care claims
- Keeping up with receipts
- Keeping home office supplies stocked
- Dispersing children's allowances
- Selecting appropriate charities
- Organizing tax information and filing return

Special Events
- Planning and coordinating birthday celebrations
- Planning and coordinating Thanksgiving and the Christmas season
- Planning and coordinating details for religious holidays and other holidays/celebrations such as Valentine's, Easter, Fourth of July, graduation, baby showers, and family reunions
- Decorating for holidays
- Organizing neighborhood activities
- Planning and orchestrating vacations
- Planning and overseeing garage sales
- Buying gifts
- Keeping gift-wrapping center stocked
- Planning weekend outings

Time & Scheduling
- Overseeing family calendar
- Making dental and doctor appointments
- Scheduling after-school activities
- Coordinating carpools and rides for family members
- Orchestrating morning schedule
- Doing advance work for future events
- Helping children manage time
- Securing babysitters
- Overseeing evening schedule
- Dealing with bedtimes and curfews
- Responding to invitations

Self-Management
- Taking care of self—physically, spiritually, mentally, and emotionally

a man's attention. Use the "Who's Responsible for What" list
(see pages 66–67) to show him a detailed list of the household
responsibilities. (You can download and personalize a copy of
this list at www.familymanager.com.)

The Rest of the Story

Once Dan and John had been approached in a winsome manner by Bonnie and Tracy and understood the responsibilities
that come with the role of Family Manager, they realized that some help from them in the laundry room
and the basement would go a long way in getting
their homes in shape and rebuilding their marriages. These things may seem small, but
such actions can get a relationship moving in the right direction.

> "When you're talking to someone, pretend like they have a sign around their neck that says 'Please make me feel important.'"
>
> —Ernie Owen

Marriage Builders and Marriage Busters

Many issues can tax a marriage. I encouraged Bonnie and Tracy
to make working on their marriage relationship a top priority.
Here are comments and suggestions I discussed with them.

• Seal all exits. Don't even consider divorce as an option.
Learning to really love each other takes hard work and time,
but the payoff is priceless. It's always too soon to quit.

- Keep the communication pathway clear. Spend time talking and listening to each other every day—even when you're tired.

- Share the load. Think of your marriage as a partnership. Divide responsibilities by giftedness and time availability, not tradition.

- Ask for and learn to grant forgiveness. If you do something wrong, admit it without blame or excuse and ask your partner to forgive you.

- Accept each other as mere mortals. You both achieve, and you both fail.

- Celebrate your differences. Remind yourself that no one is perfect and that your own weaknesses and strengths can complement your spouse's—giving breadth to your oneness.

- Learn to say "I love you" in ways that are meaningful to each other.

"If on consideration, one can find no faults on one's own side, then cry for mercy: for this must be a most dangerous delusion."

—C. S. Lewis

- Aggressively look for activities you both enjoy so you won't end up living in two separate worlds. Working on projects or pursuing hobbies together creates a lasting bond.

Makeover Strategies for Better Marriage Communication

PROBLEM

Your spouse's standard greeting as he comes through the front door and glances around the messy living room is, "So what did you do all day?" You are irritated because he doesn't appreciate your hard work at home and in fact expects you to do more to meet his needs.

SOLUTION

Schedule time to talk with your husband alone. Before bringing up your feelings, listen to his. Then tell him your goal is to be a good wife, mother, and Family Manager. Show him the "Who's Responsible for What" list. Talk about how you can work together to make your home run more smoothly.

PROBLEM

Your husband spends little time helping out with housecleaning, cooking, or caring for your children.

SOLUTION

Take time to discuss your need for help and why he hasn't done more to assist you. Perhaps he felt he'd be intruding on your territory, so he backed off. Maybe he has tried in the past and your standards were so high he felt frustrated and scolded rather than appreciated for his effort.

PROBLEM

You find yourself trying to make your husband feel guilty for refusing to step up and help around the house. You're frustrated by his uncooperative attitude.

SOLUTION

Trying to manipulate him using guilt usually worsens the situation. Instead, thank him any time you catch him helping out around the house. Also, consider that many men like options. Rather than ordering him to do something, give him a list of chores and ask him to select several to complete.

GOAL: *Solicit your spouse's help and support within your household.*

PROBLEM

While it's perfectly obvious to you what needs to be done around the house, your husband seems totally oblivious. You get tired of telling him to do the same things over and over again.

SOLUTION

Besides being gracious and patient (and putting duct tape over your mouth) when you're appalled at his inability to see what needs to be done, keep in mind that this is not his full-time territory. There are areas in all of our lives where we don't operate up to each other's expectations.

PROBLEM

You've come to see your spouse as little more than your backup in managing one crisis after another in your household. You seldom interact unless you're dealing with a problem.

SOLUTION

If you find yourself resenting your husband or appreciating him only for the help he offers around the house, be careful. Such an attitude will erode your marriage little by little. Begin consciously giving to your marriage, whether by scheduling a monthly date night or committing to regularly exercise or pray together.

PROBLEM

You feel like your marriage is in trouble but don't know what to do.

SOLUTION

Ask your husband if he would be willing to go with you to a marriage counselor. If your husband is not willing to go, you can still gain insight from a counselor on your own. Ask your pastor or friends with similar values for references of good counselors in your area.

- Give each other space for different interests. When you individually pursue various hobbies, friendships, and careers, you become more interesting to each other as you share what you've experienced.

- Invest in counseling, if necessary. When you get dangerously close to the crash-and-burn stage in your marriage, step back, take stock of the situation, and remind yourself that a good marriage doesn't just happen. It takes not only time but also a lot of work and patience.

- Remember that love is a verb; act on it every day. Put it on your Daily Hit List (see page 179).

- Don't stop dating. Book your babysitter ahead of time for two or three date nights each month. Jealously guard this time together.

- Plan at least two getaways a year without the kids—even if it's only for two or three days. Every couple needs time away together.

- Set aside some time once a month to meet and discuss your schedules and family goals.

- Be intellectually stimulating. Introduce each other to new books, hobbies, and ideas regularly.

- Never go to bed angry. Keep talking.

Seeing Eye to Eye

What do you do when you see a perfect day to clean out the garage and your husband sees his only opportunity to play golf for the next three weeks because he's taking several business trips? when you see a disaster zone in the basement and he sees a project in progress? when you see a to-do list with twenty-five items on it (many with his initials behind them) and he sees the play-off schedule? What do you do when you see a sloppily cleaned kitchen with pots and pans in the sink, and he sees a job satisfactorily accomplished?

You stop, sit down, think about the place you're in, and pray that God will help you decide what's important and what's not. If it's an issue that needs to be discussed, ask God to help you share your feelings without blame and unkind words.

- Listen to inspirational messages or audio books together when you're in the car. Talk about what you are learning.

- Pray together regularly. Keep developing that spiritual bond.

- Exercise together often. Encourage each other to live a healthy lifestyle.

In addition to encouraging Bonnie and Tracy to communicate more effectively with their husbands, I gave them some suggestions for resolving their household frustrations. Good executive managers understand the importance of continuing education to keep up with new ideas and strategies in their industry and learn how to manage better. The same was true for Bonnie and Tracy. Bonnie needed to excavate her laundry room so the clean laundry didn't have to be spread all over the family room. She also needed to declutter and organize the rest of her house, room by room. Tracy needed to get the basement cleared out and create a plan for storing her children's toys. As both moms well knew, it's hard to get a lot done with three young children in tow, and they were both waiting for a large block of time to tackle industrial-size chores. I suggested they stop waiting for a large block of uninterrupted time—a precious commodity in a house of five—to work on decluttering and organization.

Both moms could take advantage of five minutes here and there to get jobs done. Tracy could take garbage sacks and plastic storage bins downstairs and fill them when a few minutes appeared, steadily chipping away at the piles. Bonnie could apply the same strategy to organizing her kitchen, children's rooms, and other clutter hot spots. Overwhelming areas will eventually be tamed when you work in short spurts. (For more ideas on controlling clutter, see chapter 9.)

Personal Reflection

Any of us can get dangerously close to a breakdown in our marriage before we realize we're desperate. If your marital relationship has deteriorated to the point where you are enduring rather than enjoying each other, remember that God doesn't want you just to tolerate each other. He desires for you to have a rich and fulfilling relationship, and with His help this can happen.

"Grant that I may not so much seek to be . . . understood as to understand." —Saint Francis of Assisi

Have you tried to understand your husband, or do you focus on how he doesn't understand you? Are there issues about which you need to ask his forgiveness, even if you feel as though he's more to blame? Mending relational rifts is essential to a healthy marriage. Healing takes time, but you can do something today to start the process.

If you're a single mom, consider how you might draw on some of the principles in this chapter to communicate your needs to other family members, friends, or perhaps even your ex-spouse.

> **Man does not live by words alone, despite the fact that sometimes he has to eat them.**

Adlai Stevenson

> **I have oft regretted my speech—never my silence.**

Publilius Syrus

> **Do everything without complaining or arguing, so that you may become blameless and pure, children of God without fault in a crooked and depraved generation, in which you shine like stars in the universe as you hold out the word of life.**

Philippians 2:14–16

CHAPTER 5

Family Teamwork Makeover

How to Reduce Your Need to Nag

Got family? Then chances are good there's an annoying habit or two that's bugging you. If you're like many women, that habit—though small and often inconsequential—sends your nag-o-meter's mercury rising. Whether it's dirty clothes on the bathroom floor, mail all over the countertop, dirty dishes in the family room, or kids who don't pitch in around the house, nagging is often a knee-jerk reaction to our frustration. There have been many issues over the years that have set me off.

For example, Bill had a ratty T-shirt that he loved to wear around the house. I despised his routine of coming home from work and trading a crisp, white button-down for the faded, holey, laundered-to-the-threads T-shirt. It was an eyesore for me but ideal for working on household projects since he needn't worry about getting it dirty or torn. Yet day after day, this flipped my nag switch.

Silly, isn't it? Here he was actually tending to work that needed to be done around the house, and I was still complaining. You'd think I could have overlooked the stupid T-shirt and shown some gratitude that he was fixing things. Good grief! It wasn't like he was wearing it out to dinner. I'm not proud of the fact that I threw it away one day when he was out, nor am I sure why I made an issue out of it, but I'm sure selfish immaturity and pride came into play.

Then there were times when "How do I nag thee; let me count the ways" was a perfect line for me—especially when we were expecting company. Major Mom wanted our home perfect before the guests arrived, and I wanted it to stay that way during their visit. I nagged away trying to make this happen, but with three boys this was an unrealistic expectation if the guests stayed more than five minutes.

Despite the family-team mentality we adopted early on, I often backslid into gotta-be-perfect mode, making my family crazy with self-imposed rules about how my house, my schedule, and my family should run. Notice all those possessive pronouns: *my, my, my*. It was my way or the highway—not a good plan for creating a happy home.

You know, my pediatrician always told me that children go through stages, but my experience tells me that parents do too. My family will bear witness that my lapses in and out of stages when I drove myself to be Super-Mom and Ms. Perfect Homemaker were not happy times.

Girlfriend, would you be stand-in-front-of-the-mirror-in-a-bathing-suit honest and admit that there are times when you expect your family to read your mind? I confess that I sure do.

Conflict cannot survive without your participation.

You know what I mean. We say we don't care where we go out for dinner and then accuse our family members of being insensitive when they choose a greasy hamburger joint. They ask us what they can do to help, and we get irritated because we think they should know what to do without asking—then nag them when they don't do it right. This is simply not fair.

And while we're standing in front of the mirror, let's admit that one of the reasons our husbands and children don't want to hear what we say is because we don't speak in ways that make them want to listen. After all, who wants to listen to a person who's constantly nagging, complaining, or criticizing? Or a person who wants you to listen but doesn't want to listen to you? Or a person who uses his or her tongue to inflict pain?

Nagging, critical words and complaints over things that in the grand scheme of life really aren't all that important can poison the atmosphere of our homes—and if not checked, can put family relationships in jeopardy. If you've fallen into the habit of nagging, there will never be a better time than now to stop because (a) nagging is a poor motivator, so you're wasting your breath; (b) it doesn't inspire people to cooperate, so you're defeating your own purpose; and (c) it can downgrade the atmosphere in your home quicker than you can say, "If I've told you once, I've told you a thousand times." In other words, nobody wins.

Sonia's Story

When I met Sonia, she was a veteran at nagging. Fortunately, though, she knew she was a nagger and didn't want to be one. The mother of three children, ages six, eight, and ten, Sonia was one busy lady. She worked full-time as an office manager and was also earning a master's degree in business. In addition to her full-time job and course work, she was up to her eyeballs in daily to-dos around the house.

When she left home in the morning, she often wrote lists for her kids about chores that needed to be done that day after school. It perturbed her to come home at night and walk into a kitchen that wasn't cleaned to her specifications or go upstairs and find a halfheartedly made bed. She felt as though some days all she did was badger her children—for their own good, of course—about one thing or another.

Sonia's husband had a demanding job and schedule as well. To make matters worse, he and his brother grew up in a home where their mother cleaned house with a vengeance and "loved to care for her men." (Translation: The guys didn't lift a finger.)

> An unspoken expectation is an impossible expectation.

Sonia shared with me a fear common among moms: She

was worried that her family was starting to think of her as a nag. She desperately wanted her kids to have happy childhood memories—not memories of a mom who was constantly hounding them to clean up, pick up, help out, be responsible, yada, yada, yada. But Sonia felt stuck. On one hand, she hated all the nagging. On the other hand, she hated feeling like everyone's personal maid. Like Karen in chapter 3, she wanted a clean home—but the home of a family of five is too much work for one busy mom alone.

Sonia and I discussed the power of words, the importance of learning to communicate in positive ways, and a plan for getting her husband and kids to help out more around the house—without nagging them. We created a notebook that became her family's Standard Operating Procedures manual for the home. I explained that a Family Manager doesn't always get her way about everything, and if she wanted to build a family team and get some help around the house, then her husband and children needed to feel part of the process from the beginning.

Sonia and her family worked together to create their SOP manual. They made one page for each room in their home and wrote a specific definition of what *clean* meant for each room. They discussed, negotiated, and answered questions such as:

- What does cleaning up after dinner entail?

- How often should bed linens be changed?

Makeover Strategies for Encouraging Team Spirit

PROBLEM

The atmosphere has become negative in your home. Kind and loving words are not the norm. You want things to change.

SOLUTION

Own up to your part of the problem. Apologize to family members if you have been a nag or overly negative. Tell them you want to create a more positive atmosphere. Talk about ways you can work together to make home a more pleasant place.

PROBLEM

In order to get your kids to help at all around the house, you feel your only choice is to nag. Yet even that doesn't seem to be getting any results.

SOLUTION

Take a step back and listen to yourself. Is it possible your family tunes you out because you sound unceasingly critical? Try a one-to-five approach: for every one time you have to reprimand or give negative input to family members, be alert for five ways you can praise or give positive input to them.

PROBLEM

It is difficult to get your children to cooperate, and it seems that they only respond after you've laid down the law.

SOLUTION

You may have fallen into a negative-attention cycle, in which children don't cooperate as a way to get your attention. Expect your children to obey the first time you ask them to do something. Remember, your authority does not increase with volume or repetition. Impose consequences for noncooperation.

GOAL: *Put an end to nagging and work together as a family to create a home that lives up to standards you have agreed on.*

PROBLEM

You don't think your definition of *clean* is unreasonable, but based on your kids' reaction whenever you ask them to pitch in with housework, you've decided *clean* isn't even in their vocabulary.

SOLUTION

Meet with your family to talk about your standards for each room in the house. Work together to create a "Standard Operating Procedures" notebook or just a document that includes agreed-upon criteria for how clean each room in your house will be. (It's important to put it in writing so everyone will remember the standards you agreed on.)

PROBLEM

As you're starting dinner, you hear your kids bickering in the family room. Without looking, you're pretty sure they must be arguing over whose turn it is to play on the computer.

SOLUTION

Watch for recurring areas of conflict, and then take a few minutes to establish firm guidelines. For example, keep a timer near the computer and set it for a specific amount of time for each child's turn. When the buzzer goes off, it's the other child's turn to play. Failure to comply means they don't get to play.

PROBLEM

No matter how often you remind your son to put his socks in the hamper, every day you seem to discover another pair of dirty socks somewhere else—under his desk, by the TV, or in the bathroom. Whenever you spot a pair, you feel your emotional temperature start to rise.

SOLUTION

Teaching your kids good habits is a process, not a one-time event. Look for opportunities to get your child to take personal responsibility. You might place any socks found on the floor in "sock jail." When he runs out of socks, he may have to wear dad's "old man" socks to school—an unbearable consequence for our guys.

83

- What areas of our home should be clutter-free zones?

- What does a clean closet look like?

- How often do floors need to be swept?

- What's the definition of a clean garage?

These answers and more were recorded in their SOP manual. The manual also established consequences when agreed-upon standards weren't met. When it was time to clean the kitchen, the notebook was there for review.

"Do not let any unwholesome talk come out of your mouths, but only what is helpful for building others up according to their needs, that it may benefit those who listen."
(Ephesians 4:29)

Identifying and negotiating expectations reduced Sonia's need to nag—and everyone liked that! She was able to let go of some of her high expectations without relinquishing her desire for a clean home. "It's not as clean as I would like, but that's okay because my family is doing more and I'm nagging less," Sonia said.

Marketing Your Cause

It's a well-known business principle that workers who buy into the company's goals are more likely to work to meet those goals. So at home, start by talking with your family about expectations. What do you—that would be the plural *you*, everyone in your family who can talk—expect? This might include everything from an orderly home to eating dinner together most nights to keeping everyone in clean clothes.

> "Govern a family as you would cook a small fish: very gently."
>
> —*Chinese proverb*

If you approach your family with the notion of teamwork and find it's a hard sell, consider that your family might be hearing you say that you only want their help doing things *your* way—according to your expectations. If this is the case, you will need to rethink your wants and your ways. What are your husband's goals? your children's? How could working together as a team help each of you meet your individual goals? Find ways to mesh each person's expectations with the family goal of an efficiently running, fun home. For example, you might tell your son, "After you clean up downstairs on Friday, you can call your friends and invite them over after the game."

If you're tired of bickering with your kids, I encourage you to try positive motivation instead of nagging or yelling. This leads only to frustration for everyone. Children respond in different ways to various types of positive motivation—tangible rewards, checklists, verbal praise, games, and challenges. Think about what types of incentives spur your children on. If one method fails, try another. The important thing is to be patient and keep trying. The end result—responsible, self-disciplined children—is well worth the effort.

Also, be willing to negotiate. What's spick and span to one person may be filthy to another. Everyone has a different tolerance level for dirt. I think there's a lot of truth in the old adage "Home should be clean enough to be healthy and dirty enough to be happy." In other words, I don't know of anyone who likes bugs crawling on their countertops. But on the other hand, who cares if the sink's gleaming if Mom's always playing chief nag?

> "Where there is no vision, the people perish."
> (Proverbs 29:18, KJV)

Come up with your family's definition of *clean*. Be specific, and let everyone have a say. Describe what each room looks like when it's clean. This means everyone will probably have to give a little (and maybe in some cases a lot), but that's what being a family and a team is about. In my experience, this is an eye-opening exercise, mainly because you, the Family Manager, see things that others take for granted. Maybe your teenager will give a general description of how he likes the bathroom: clean. Maybe he has never thought about why there is or isn't mildew in the shower or what that funny little brush is in the container behind the toilet. Coming up with a definition of *clean* is a good springboard for discussion and a good way to start the process of delegating the chores it takes to maintain your shared definition of *clean*.

Do Yourself—and Your Kids—
a Favor

You're doing your kids a favor when you require them to help out at home. They learn life skills—like running a washing machine and a vacuum cleaner. You also teach them cooperation and collaboration skills that will serve them in any walk of life. Delegating also helps balance the workloads between marriage partners. And it builds on the idea that home belongs to everyone; therefore, everyone contributes to its care.

Many parents wonder what to do when their kids won't cooperate. If you can relate to their problem, consider these questions: Does your son or daughter watch TV? play video or computer games? enjoy using favorite toys or electronic devices?

Those activities, and others like them, are *privileges*, not *rights*. We do our kids a favor when we have a policy that says: Until you fulfill your responsibilities, you do not get your privileges. Granted, kids won't like this—but they'll bow to it if you stand firm.

Even more important than your children's cooperation is the lesson they learn about real life. After all, that's the way the adult world operates. If you don't fulfill your responsibilities for your job, you won't have the privilege of getting a paycheck or maybe even having a job at all. Your child deserves to learn this at home, where the stakes are small, rather than in the cold, cruel world, where the stakes are enormous.

Be supportive and express confidence in your team's ability to do a good job. Your positive expectations and praise when the job is done often set the stage for higher performance and create a more positive relationship between you and your team members. Thank your family for every task they do, even if it's something you expect of them. Gratitude is always in order.

Continue to solicit input from family members, and listen, listen, listen. Let each person talk openly and honestly about what makes him or her feel unvalued as a team member. Talk about what would have to happen for those feelings to change. Make sure everyone knows that you're committed to each family member's best interest. You're not attempting to make them miserable or burden them with extra responsibilities. You're simply trying to make everyone's life a little easier by spreading out the work more evenly.

Barking orders is for controlling marine platoons and packs of dogs. Asking nicely goes a lot further than demanding.

If you've been a nag, maybe it's time for you to sit down with your family and ask forgiveness—even if you think you're only 5 percent of the problem. Take responsibility and admit your own mistakes. Without blaming, confirm your love and confess that you want to be a good Family Manager—not a nag.

And remember: No one has ever been or ever will be a perfect Family Manager. What's important is that we keep trying to be better. What we do every day will determine what our homes will be like in the years to come and what our kids will remember when they leave home. Hopefully they'll remember that home was a place they loved to be and Mom was a fun person to be around.

Personal Reflection

Some families live in the midst of civil war. What began as seemingly harmless nagging grew into unkind words, which grew into critical words, which grew into spiteful, harsh words. Now their homes are like war zones. Family members live as if they are enemies. Words are their weapons. Battles are often bloody, casualty rates are high, and children are innocent victims. No one wins and everybody loses unless someone decides that things have to change—which they can. It only takes one person who's willing to move toward peace and begin reconstruction.

"Reckless words pierce like a sword, but the tongue of the wise brings healing." (Proverbs 12:18)

Have you spoken any words to your family that may have pierced like a sword? What will you do today to begin the peacemaking process?

66 **Early morning hath gold in its mouth.** 99

Benjamin Franklin

---

66 **Day's sweetest moments are at dawn.** 99

Ella Wheeler Wilcox

---

66 **With God all things are possible.** 99

Mark 10:27, KJV

✳

CHAPTER 6

Morning Routine Makeover

Turning Chaos into Calm

Calm. Cool. Collected. Those aren't words you normally find on the same page—let alone the same paragraph—as the word *morning*. That's because for many moms, morning is the least relaxing time of day. It's a shame, really, and a bit of a contradiction too. After all, we've just woken up from a restful sleep and should feel ready to meet the day's challenges. But women across the country report that this just isn't so. Instead of creating a peaceful, reflective period for ourselves, we anticipate mornings with dread and then struggle through them.

As Family Managers, we play a vitally important role in shaping the way our families greet the morning. Mornings set the tone for the day. We can lovingly wake our children and launch them into the world from a peaceful, positive environment, or we can invite chaos to have a seat at our breakfast table.

At our house, the year John (our first child) started kindergarten proved to be a unique kind of wake-up call. I knew attending school would be a major turning point in his young life, but I never dreamed it would also be one for me. During his first several weeks of school, I started the day by pushing the snooze button three or four times in order to linger under the covers a little longer. Then—at the last possible moment (thirty minutes before school started, with a ten-minute drive to the building)—I'd rush into John's room and wake him up.

Habitually behind on laundry, I often selected John's attire based on what smelled the least offensive. I'd frantically sort through the pile of dirty clothes, sniffing and tossing as I went along, until I came across something acceptable. While he dressed, I bolted to the kitchen to prepare breakfast. Many days, there was an empty place on the bottom shelf of the refrigerator where a gallon of milk should have been. I tried to lessen John's disappointment over being served another bowl of dry cereal by using creative diversion. "John, I have a fun idea! Let's pretend our spaceship crashed on the moon and there's nothing to eat but dried food." But John was on to me. "Mom," my wise-beyond-his-years five-year-old would ask suspiciously, "are we out of milk again?"

"Never mind," I'd snap as I watched him devour the most important meal of the day void of proper nutrition. With each passing second I grew more nervous, checking the clock frequently. "Hurry up, honey, you don't have all day! The carpool will be here any minute."

When the horn sounded, I'd rush him out the door and gently shove him into my friend's car. (The clock was really ticking now.) My friend and I exchanged knowing glances. We were so grateful for radar detectors. That's right. I'm ashamed to admit it, but it's true. We relied on radar detectors to get our kids to school on time. Sad, isn't it?

As her station wagon sped off, I prayed that despite the rough start, John would have a good day. Reflecting on my own early school years, I remembered how stressful school can be for children. All those rules and routines can feel so overwhelming.

Luckily for my family, it didn't take me long to realize that this was no way to manage a morning! The desperation I felt seemed to propel me to a new place. I was suddenly ready to meet the challenge. I knew I wanted our day to begin peacefully and positively, but I didn't know

> "Things do not change, we change."
> —Henry David Thoreau

how to move from chaos to calm. So I did what I always do when I don't know what else to do . . . I prayed. I prayed that my utter lack of organization hadn't permanently damaged my son. I prayed that we'd no longer wake up to cereal without milk, and I prayed I could get the kids to school on time without the aid of illegal devices! And God, just one more thing. . . . Please show this hard-core night owl how to become a morning person.

Strange as it seems, it was the first chapter of Genesis that renewed my sense of hope. I read that in the beginning the earth was formless and void of order and God turned it into something beautiful and orderly. My home and life seemed pretty formless and void of order, so I asked God to do the same for me.

It didn't happen overnight, but praying myself out of bed in the morning seemed to jump-start the process. I didn't like getting up, so I just asked God to help me do it—not to make me like doing it. Before long, I saw that I was at least part of the answer to my prayer. Too much useless, late-night TV was interfering with a reasonable bedtime and making me grouchy in the morning. Hmmm . . . if I went to bed earlier, I reasoned, then I might be able to wake up earlier.

Then, after I ran out of milk for the umpteenth time, I started making a list to help me remember to replenish the food supply. You get the picture. Needless to say, my family loved the changes. Having a cheerful mom was a big bonus. Everyone seemed more relaxed, thanks to the slower pace of the morning, and eating something other than astronaut food for breakfast was a big hit too.

Postscript: Mornings became my favorite part of the day. They were *my* time, and although my new routine started early—5:45 a.m.—hitting the snooze button was no longer a

The Right Start to Your Day

Mornings are the launching pad for the day. One of our most important jobs as the manager of our family is to see that the day starts off right, with positive communication and a calm environment. Life is challenging enough without adding impatient words and a frenzied atmosphere to the mix—all because we weren't prepared to meet the day. I've heard mothers, fathers, and kids alike tell me that mornings have become so unpleasant that instead of leaving the office or school and looking forward to going home at the end of the day, they want to escape someplace else to avoid more stress. It doesn't need to be this way.

How are mornings at your house? Do your children leave for school nourished in mind, body, and spirit, or do they start the day with a deficit?

problem. The appeal of a quiet cup of coffee and some unhurried time with God got me vertical on most days. I relished reading from the Bible and various devotional books, and

> "Morning is when I am awake and there is a dawn in me."
>
> —Henry David Thoreau

writing in my prayer journal. Then, as the day was dawning, I wrote out my to-dos (which eventually evolved into the Family Manager Daily Hit List, which you can read about in chapter 10). Each day had a purpose, and making a list kept me focused and helped me accomplish my goals. By the time the boys got up at 6:45, I felt renewed. Starting the day like this helped me immensely. I lovingly greeted my family, and we all started the day on a positive note.

Although I still had a long way to go in Family Manager departments like Home and Property, Finances, and Food, this was an important first step, and it motivated me to get organized in other areas of my life. Recently, Family Manager Coach Sandra Forbes shared with me the details of her experience, which resulted in her learning much the same lesson.

Sandra's Story

Sandra—wife, mother of six, and volunteer extraordinaire—is one of those high-octane women who makes you want to know the secret of her get-up-and-go. Within a few seconds of meeting her, you can sense her cheerful, energetic spirit and can-do approach to life! But here's the reality . . . even high-octane women like Sandra go through difficult times, lose perspective, and become desperate to regain the energy and positive outlook on life they once enjoyed. See if you don't recognize yourself in at least some part of the following story.

"When I think about last year, I think of chaos," said Sandra. "In addition to homeschooling four of our six children and overseeing cooking, cleaning, laundry, and the countless other responsibilities that come with running a large household, we were in the midst of extensive renovations on our home."

During the renovations, her family lived in one small area of the house. The baby slept in his parents' room, and the other children shared a room, with one of them sleeping on a mattress on the floor. Every morning Sandra had to pick up the mattress and move it out of the way so they could get to the only working bathroom. A camper trailer in the driveway served as their kitchen, and all meals were cooked and eaten there.

Thankfully, the main renovations were completed just before the start of a new school year. This meant the family could move back into their "new" house and start school all at the same time. New beginnings were usually invigorating for Sandra, but this time she found her vigor waning. As the weeks wore on, she became less and less productive during schooltime. The ongoing work on the house was weighing heavily on her. Overwhelmed by responsibilities and a house that never seemed "together," Sandra soon found herself in a state of constant exhaustion and less responsive to her family's needs.

Surprisingly, it was at this point that Sandra decided to begin hosting a Bible study in her home. "One of the things I had always wanted to do but had never allowed myself to do was attend a Bible study. I decided to put aside my pride that my house was still under construction and not perfect and host a Bible study. I figured that if we met at my house, my older children could help watch the other women's younger children. The Bible study wouldn't just be 'my' thing, but more of a family effort. As it happened, the Bible study refreshed me in ways I never expected," she said. "Hosting my 'want-to' Bible study at our home seemed to multiply my energy on other days to complete my 'have-tos.'"

To make her new schedule work, which now included homeschooling and a weekly Bible study conducted within a home undergoing renovation, Sandra knew the first hours of her day would be critical. "If I fell behind in the morning, I would be behind all day," she said.

Sandra felt that the very first hour was the most important, so she decided to spend this time in prayer and study. She also knew that the house was a huge distraction for her, so she scheduled enough time to get the house straightened before she started schoolwork with her kids. "This helped me minimize the numerous temptations to stop for 'just a sec' to clean something," she said. "Although the school day started a little later than before, I was able to accomplish more with the children since I didn't have the little here-and-there cleaning interruptions. Plus, the kids benefited from a more cheerful mother!"

"God helped me see that if I wanted to free myself from the attitudes and habits that were prohibiting me from living and enjoying a balanced life, I needed to create boundaries for myself in the form of a schedule. Sounds crazy, yet I knew from experience that discipline brings freedom. All of a sudden everything in my life began to make sense. No wonder I ended up in an emotional pit!" said Sandra.

"Now, with renewed hope, I began to think of ways I could reorder my daily schedule and get my life back on track. I could

> "It's not that some people have willpower and some don't. It's that some people are ready to change and others are not."
> —James Gordon, M.D.

feel my energy returning when I realized the freedom my new schedule would afford me: freedom to say no to unimportant interruptions, freedom to say no to volunteer opportunities that don't fit with our family's plans and priorities, freedom to say yes to some things I wanted to do but hadn't allowed myself to do."

From her Bible study, Sandra also discovered the freedom

that comes from letting others see that you don't have every area of your life together. "Since the study began before my kitchen was installed, each week the women who attended got to watch the kitchen unfold and my house come together. Actually, I think they felt even more comfortable than if my house had been perfect—which it never will be anyway! As a family, our vision for our home to be a place of welcome and ministry was coming alive before the work was even finished."

What about You?

What are mornings like at your house? Are you constantly running late and getting frustrated over the same things, day after day, week after week? Do you stay up until the wee hours of the morning and cower at the thought of getting up earlier? Sandra and I are living proof that night owls can become morning people. If we can do it, you can too!

No matter what your body clock says right now, you need to give your kids a good start to the day. We all have to do things we don't like, and changing our attitudes about doing those things can sometimes make us like them. When I first started getting out of bed earlier in the morning, I did it because I had to. God helped me. Then one day I found that I actually liked doing it. Of course, we don't always end up liking everything we have to do. I never hear people talking about how much they like to clean bathrooms—but we all like having clean

Rework Your Body Clock

Only you know how much rest you need. Some women can't function without eight hours of sleep. Some do fine on six. But when it comes to getting out of bed earlier than we might like, eventually we all have to do the math.

Change begins by taking some small steps.

- *Decide* you're going to become a morning person. Repeat out loud, over and over, "I am a morning person. I start the day off right for myself and my family." If this sounds silly to you, do it anyway. The message will become planted in your subconscious mind.

- Take a long, hot soak in the tub before bed. This starts the relaxation process.

- Turn off the television at least thirty minutes before bed.

- View your bedroom as a place to rest and relax only. Make your bed as comfortable as possible. If your pillow is uncomfortable, replace it.

- Start the habit of reading the Bible or a good book just before you turn off the light. Fill your mind with positive thoughts to pave the way for a peaceful night's rest.

- Set two alarms (one battery powered). Keep one in the bathroom so you have to get out of bed to turn it off. Program your coffeepot so your coffee will be ready when you are.

- Get out of your jammies ASAP in the morning.

- Create a comfortable spot in your home where you can start the day with God.

Makeover Strategies for Smoother Mornings

PROBLEM

After staying up late frantically trying to complete housework and other responsibilities, you wake up tired.

SOLUTION

Determine how many hours of sleep you need to wake up refreshed the next day. Based on that number, figure out what time you need to get to bed. That may mean working with your spouse to establish earlier bedtime routines for the kids. (Be sure to work in some exclusive couple time after they're in bed.)

PROBLEM

From the time your feet hit the floor, you are rushing to respond to someone else's need.

SOLUTION

Schedule time alone with God before anyone else wakes up. You might read your Bible, pray, and write in a prayer journal. It's also a great time to draft a to-do list for the day. Once you begin spending time seeking God's direction for the day, you won't want to sacrifice the peace it brings.

PROBLEM

You waste time in the mornings trying to help your kids find something to wear.

SOLUTION

Ask your kids to set out their clothes the night before. (Packing away all items that don't fit or are out of season will simplify choices.) If your kids like to decide in the morning, hang all school clothes in one area of the closet and build wardrobes around basic color bottoms that will coordinate with a wide variety of tops.

GOAL: *Start your family's mornings off on positive footing.*

PROBLEM
Your family never seems to have time for breakfast, but you know it's important and want to make it a priority.

SOLUTION
Set the table for breakfast the night before. Provide simple "no cooking" foods like cereal (offer only two choices), bagels, fruit, and juice. Sit down at the table together even if it's just for five minutes to talk about your kids' day. This is a great time to double-check schedules and find out if they'll need anything at the store that day.

PROBLEM
Phone calls and e-mail begin to intrude on your family time as you begin each day.

SOLUTION
Record a new phone message explaining that you are unavailable before noon each weekday but will respond to messages in the afternoon. Set aside one or two specific times during the day to read and respond to e-mail.

PROBLEM
You often find yourself spending precious minutes hunting for your keys or purse in the morning.

SOLUTION
Designate a basket, shelf, or hooks by your door where you always place your keys, purse, and sunglasses, as well as items for errands (like library books or dry cleaning).

bathrooms. Focusing on the fact that we like the result can go a long way in helping us change our attitude about what we're doing.

Add Hours to Your Day

I have a theory about managing and multiplying the hours of my day. A few years ago I heard a sermon about giving the firstfruits of your income to God. This certainly wasn't the first message I'd heard on tithing, but this time the subject hit me in a completely different way. I started thinking about

> "When you cannot do as you like, the best thing is to like what you have to do."
> —*George MacDonald*

God being the provider of *all* our resources—food to eat, air to breathe, water to drink, relationships to enjoy, work to do—*everything*, including our time. Every day that we wake up breathing means that He has given us the gift of another day and the resource of the hours of that day to do what He wants us to accomplish.

My habit of starting the day with God was ingrained, but I wondered if I looked at this time as more of an offering— giving God the firstfruits of my day and spending more time praying and listening to Him through the Bible—if He would bless my offering and, in a sense, give me more time back that day. I didn't want to be rigid about my experiment, but I had to start somewhere, so I began by doing some simple math.

I calculated that there are twenty-four hours in a day, and if I sleep (or *should* sleep) eight hours a day, then I have sixteen hours of awake time. I decided to dedicate 10 percent of this time—roughly one and a half hours—to my experiment.

It's nothing short of a miracle how God began to bless this time and give me back more time to accomplish the other things He wanted me to do. I don't mean He added a couple of hours to the clock after noon so that I could schedule meetings and accomplish tasks from thirteen to fifteen o'clock. Instead, I think that by starting the day in this frame of mind, seeing it as His day and time in the first place, offering myself and asking Him to give me wisdom and guidance to do His will, I am able, by His strength, to accomplish more.

> "I have so much work to do that if I didn't spend at least three hours a day in prayer, I would never get it all done."
> —Martin Luther

Perhaps by beginning the day this way, I can better see that all of what I do is really His work, and I can enjoy His help in doing it. Maybe it's that I make more good decisions and fewer bad ones so I don't waste as much time redoing things. Maybe because I'm reminded from the get-go that all my time and energy belong to God, I have better discernment about when to say no to requests for my time and when to allow things to interrupt me. Or maybe it's that I'm actually doing fewer things, but they're the right things. I can't tell you exactly why this works. I just know that by offering God the firstfruits of the day, I get more done and things run more smoothly. Not perfect, mind you, but much, much better.

I encourage you to try this experiment yourself. But don't be hung up on the amount of time you spend. Just make sure it's enough time to launch yourself into the day with the calm assurance that God is there to guide you, empower you, and walk with you, no matter what comes your way.

"In the morning, O LORD, you hear my voice; in the morning I lay my requests before you and wait in expectation."
(Psalm 5:3)

You know, much like the waves of the sea, a day looks one way when it's coming toward us, another way when we are in the midst of it, and another way when it is past. How we begin the day impacts all three perspectives.

You may have to try a few different methods before you settle into morning routines that feel right for you. And on the days when you're feeling particularly desperate, don't forget: You and God are in this together.

Personal Reflection

I don't know about you, but my emotional tank gets empty when, like my father puts it, I'm running around like a chicken with its head cut off, trying to be all things to all people. Only God can meet everyone's needs. If we want to be good Family Managers,

our first and foremost responsibility is to develop our relationship with God—getting to know Him (and ourselves) better each
day. If we do this, we'll be better prepared and equipped to love
our husbands, parent our children, and manage our homes.

"Be still before the LORD and wait patiently for him."
(Psalm 37:7)

"Give ear and come to me; hear me, that your soul may live."
(Isaiah 55:3)

Is your life ever really quiet, so that you can just sit, wait, and
listen for God? Try to spend time in prayer and read a portion of
the Bible every morning so you start the day trusting in your life-
changing God.

> **Every new day begins with possibilities. It's up to us to fill it with the things that move us toward progress and peace.**
> Ronald Reagan

> **She watches over the affairs of her household and does not eat the bread of idleness.**
> Proverbs 31:27

> **Change the name and the tale is about you.**
> Horace

※

CHAPTER 7

School Day Makeover

First Aid for Frazzled Families

....

The dictionary definition of *frazzled* is to be upset or in a state of extreme physical or nervous fatigue. And believe you me, this is a word with which our family of five is familiar. When our boys were growing up, we created mounds of dirty clothes and dishes, and always had a home improvement project going. During some seasons my schedule had more practices, meetings, and errands than the day is long.

But if I could share only one part of our family's management, it wouldn't be the way we divided up chores or saved money by painting our house by ourselves or shared carpool duties. It would be the ways we learned to relieve stress and create a positive atmosphere in our home. More than almost anything else, families desperately need this today. Grace's family sure did. Here's their story.

Grace's Story

School days at Grace and Mike's house were chaotic, to put it mildly. Grace's alarm sounded at 5:30 a.m., and she was usually out of bed by 6:00 to pack lunches for her three elementary-age children, take care of last-minute homework crises, get the kids out the door, *and* get herself ready for work. Some mornings she would realize she didn't have the right ingredients for lunch, so she'd frantically run to the grocery store before Mike left for work at 6:30.

While she bustled around the house, the kids moved slowly. She had to yell a few times to urge them to hurry and get ready. Once downstairs, they lingered over their cereal and watched cartoons. "Every morning," she said, "there's at least one surprise. One of the kids has a form that needs to be signed or a homework assignment that's not completed." Also, every morning the kids spent time rummaging through a huge basket of laundry, searching for gym clothes or matching socks.

One morning I arrived at Grace's house at 6:00 a.m. for a firsthand observation of her family's morning routines, and I can testify that it was a major ordeal to get everyone dressed, fed, and out the door. Grace was often late for work, and although he didn't say so, I think Mike was glad that he could escape the morning fray by leaving for his work early.

Afternoons weren't any better. Grace's part-time job allowed her to be home when the school bus dropped off the kids. I watched as they bounded into the house through the front door. They shed their shoes, jackets, hats, mittens, and backpacks as they went, making a trail that ended in the family room, where they immediately turned on the TV. Grace picked up their backpacks and dug out their lunch boxes. I noticed that she threw away a lot of untouched food from each one.

After an hour or so of cartoons, interspersed with a lot of sibling bickering and visits from various neighborhood children, Grace announced it was time to do homework. Complaining ensued, so she caved in, and homework waited until after dinner.

Grace's problems, from the perspective of an outside observer, may seem relatively minor and mendable with a few changes here and there. But Grace was deep in the forest, and it was hard to see the trees—which can happen to any of us. Sometimes all we need is for someone to give us a little nudge and shed a bit of light on our situation.

Grace and I talked about what she could do to relieve school-day chaos and create a more positive atmosphere in her home. We agreed that her kids needed to shoulder some responsibility and that their family could benefit from creating some House Rules and Standard Operating Procedures. Grace worked at a dentist's office, so she understood the importance of rules and SOPs in the field of dentistry. She quickly saw that applying the same concepts at home could make things more pleasant and orderly.

House Rules

I explained to Grace how having a set of house rules that everyone agrees to abide by was a big help in creating a peaceful atmosphere in my home. This way, everyone knew what to expect and what was expected.

When parents want to know one thing they can do to get the atmosphere in their home back on track, I tell them to start here. House Rules are important tools for peaceful family living, and they benefit everyone. Parents benefit because they can stand united—"We all agreed that we wouldn't slam doors when we get angry"—when kids break the rules. Children benefit from having clear boundaries about what is and what is not allowed. It gives them a sense of security to be able to say, "This is the way we always do it at our house." We wrote our House Rules early in our family history, and although they evolved over the years as our children grew older, we still live by many of them.

> "I always wondered about where 'kingdom come' might be, since my mother threatened so many times to knock me there."
>
> —Bill Cosby

Creating your own house rules will help you maintain order and save a lot of emotional energy that otherwise would be used to fuss and argue. But there are long-term benefits as well. The relational skills your kids learn at home—such as respecting others' feelings and property—will make it easier for them to form healthy relationships with friends, college roommates, spouses, and coworkers in the future.

If you decide to write your own House Rules (which I

highly recommend), you can use our House Rules as a start-ing point—the same ones I gave to Grace as a model. Keep in mind that they need to reflect your family's priorities and goals for your home. Also, remember that you're not writing rules in stone. Your family's House Rules won't be perfect, and they'll keep changing—because kids grow, situations change, and schedules are altered.

Here are the Peel House Rules:

Rule 1: We're all in this together. The rules apply to every-one—Mom and Dad too. Kids won't buy a double standard. When you give them permission to call you on the carpet for a violation, they will feel ownership of the rules. Albert Schweitzer was right when he said, "Example isn't the most important thing; example is the only thing." We must practice what we preach.

A woman told me that her children were behaving rudely toward each other and asked for my advice. In the course of the conversation I learned that she and her hus-band were in the habit of making sarcastic, disrespectful remarks to each other. We talked about the importance of being good role models for our children. She answered her own question, then went home and asked her husband if they could agree to stop their own childish behavior. In a family meeting they confessed their less-than-optimum example to the kids. She reported back to me that the atmosphere in their home had changed remarkably for the better.

Makeover Strategies for School Day Success

PROBLEM
You can't keep your children focused on getting ready for school in the morning. They turn on the TV as soon as they wake up and when they get home from school. You then struggle to get them to turn it off.

SOLUTION
Unless you need to watch the weather report on the morning news, leave the TV off. Limit afternoon TV time as well. When they *are* watching, have kids fold laundry and match socks. Tie cooperation with an allowance. Create a chore chart and post it at kids' eye level. Reward getting up, getting ready, and completing some simple household tasks both before and after school.

PROBLEM
You struggle to get lunches made while also seeing that your kids are getting dressed and eating breakfast.

SOLUTION
Once your kids are eight or so, they should be able to pack their own lunches. Keep all supplies in a central spot and have kids make their lunches during your evening kitchen cleanup. Then store the lunches in the refrigerator. To keep PBJ sandwiches from getting mushy, spread peanut butter on both slices of bread (it acts as a sealant) before adding jelly.

PROBLEM
Every morning you seem to get out the door later than you intended.

SOLUTION
Have one child act as the "town crier." Let them rotate turns being in charge of giving everyone a ten-minute warning—ten minutes before it's time to walk out the door.

GOAL: *Work together as a family to make school days less hectic and more productive for each member of your family.*

PROBLEM
You constantly nag your kids to begin their homework, yet they often don't finish until just before bedtime—often in tears.

SOLUTION
Determine the best time for your kids to do their homework and stick to that time. Since kids often need a little time to wind down immediately after school, just before or after dinner is often a good time for kids to tackle their schoolwork.

PROBLEM
Within minutes of your kids' return home from school, the pathway from your front door to the family room is strewn with coats, mittens, and lunch boxes.

SOLUTION
Install child-level hooks by your door, one for each child. Put a small bookshelf underneath, and have one labeled plastic bin for each child on a shelf. When they come in the door after school, have them immediately hang their jackets, put mittens and hats in their bins, and bring their lunch boxes to the kitchen.

PROBLEM
At least one of your kids always seems to scramble to find missing homework or a permission slip before heading to school.

SOLUTION
Set up in-boxes on your kitchen desk or countertop. Label one for each child. Have them unload school papers and forms into their in-boxes. It's Mom's or Dad's responsibility to look at papers at night and follow through on any necessary actions.

Let kids who are old enough have a say in how rules should apply to all of you. For example, when you talk about housekeeping guidelines, a rule for everybody might be: "Don't leave wet towels on the bathroom floor." Children might want to add, "Mom, don't go ballistic when someone leaves a wet towel on the bathroom floor."

Rule 2: No yelling at anyone or "pitching fits." Reserve yelling and screaming for emergencies only. Authority does not increase with volume. Lay down the rule about yelling, and enforce the consequences. "Outside voices" are not to be used inside, and screaming at others is not tolerated. And remember, the moment you are drawn into a yelling match, you surrender parental authority to the strength of the personalities involved. When you are tempted to raise your voice in a show of authority, try thinking of something Margaret Thatcher said: "Being powerful is like being a lady. If you have to tell people you are, you aren't." If I have to raise my voice to prove I'm in authority, then I'm not.

> "It is not fair to ask of others what you are not willing to do yourself."
> —Eleanor Roosevelt

When we are emotionally wound up, our voices magnify. Be aware of this when dealing with a problem. Slow down your own speech. This will help you speak in a more gentle tone of voice.

If you're really riled and aren't sure you can control

Sleep and Your Kids

Does your child have a tough time waking up in the morning? Your child's sleep schedule impacts more than his or her mood, according to M. C. Culbertson III, MD, professor of pediatrics at the University of Connecticut School of Medicine.

Sleep helps children learn by enabling the brain to process and store information from the day. Deep sleep also triggers the release of the human growth hormone—a substance necessary for physical development and a healthy immune system. School-age kids need ten to eleven hours of shut-eye a night. Those who get less are prone to injury and illness, and they lack concentration in school.

If your kids aren't getting enough sleep, consider these solutions:

- Cut caffeine. One caffeinated beverage per day can cause kids to lose thirty minutes of sleep nightly.
- Ban TVs and computers from the bedroom. Children who have TVs in their rooms lose nearly three hours of sleep weekly.
- Make books part of the bedtime routine. Children who read or are read to are most likely to get enough sleep.
- Be alert for loud snoring, mouth breathing, and gasping that can signal sleep apnea, a condition that prevents deep sleep. Consult your child's doctor.

your feelings, take a few minutes to regroup. If you can't get away, force yourself to count to one hundred slowly. Once *you've* calmed down, you can lay down the law with the kids about talking things over calmly.

"No pitching fits" was an early rule—with consequences—when our boys were small. From an early age, children need to know this is not acceptable behavior. We had a parental guideline: We never gave the desired response when a child used pitching a fit as a means of getting it.

Rule 3: Delete the phrase "Shut up!" from our vocabulary entirely. Every human being is a uniquely made individual, worthy of respect. Don't tolerate these or other disrespectful or devaluing words between family members. Make sure everyone knows offenders will face consequences.

We taught our children that when a sibling got on their nerves or interrupted a conversation, they were allowed to say, "Please be quiet." Since kids will be kids and sometimes don't want to comply with the requests of a sibling, if the offender did not voluntarily refrain from "bugging" or talking by the third request, a judge (usually a parent) was brought in, and we sat down and talked about what was going on. Many times the offending behavior was in-

"Always and never are two words you should always remember never to use."
—Wendell Johnson

tended to annoy the brother who was asking for silence. In that case, I dealt with the annoying behavior and talked to the offender about the importance of showing preference to others above ourselves.

Rule 4: Calling names or making unkind, cutting remarks to each other is strictly off limits. There's an old saying: "To belittle is to be little." Talk to your children about the meaning of this saying. Help them understand that they're being small persons if they find it necessary to cut someone else down.

The fact that we laugh a lot with and at each other is one of the things I enjoy most about our family. But every family must have boundaries. Some comments are definitely out-of-bounds and do not fall into the category of playful teasing. It's important that when family members poke fun at one another, it's fun for everyone. It's not funny to joke about someone's big nose, deformities, seemingly stupid mistakes, fears, or weaknesses. If a comment made in a joking manner hurts feelings, be sure to talk it out so it won't happen again.

Make a list of the names and negative phrases you would like to eliminate from your family's vocabulary, like "dummy," "stupid," "punk," "I don't like you," or "You make me sick." Talk about how each person feels when these things are said to him or her. Set a family goal to rid these terms and phrases from your conversation. Put each person in charge of him- or herself. Create a chart with each person's name. Put a check mark by the name of the person who has a slip of the tongue and uses one of the off-limits words or phrases.

Rule 5: Take responsibility for our own actions and words. Children need help learning how to work through conflicts. They don't know how to do this instinctively. When your kids get into a fight, sit them down and listen to both sides of the story. Ask questions that make each one think about both sides of the problem. Guide them as they determine the root problem and focus on their behavior—not what was done to them.

Help your children learn the principle that small people blame others for their mistakes and actions. Make them aware that they are always responsible for their own actions and that you hold them responsible for their deeds—no matter what the other person does. There is no excuse for poor behavior, a poor response, or blaming someone else for our problem.

Rule 6: Ask forgiveness when we have hurt or offended someone, even if it was an accident. Sometimes it's hard for kids to see the importance of restoring a relationship—especially if they don't think they did anything wrong. It's important that we teach them to try to feel the other person's pain or discomfort. Make sure you set the example by apologizing when you hurt or disappoint them—even if it was unintentional. Saying, "I'm sorry" or "I was wrong" won't undermine your authority. Living by a double standard will.

Rule 7: Keep confidential what we share with each other. Your children need to know that they can trust you. Create a safe environment for communication. Here's an important question: When your son or daughter comes face-to-face with a temptation or difficult situation and is struggling with what to do, will he or she want to talk to you? Are you considered a safe, supportive, trustworthy, and reliable source of counsel?

The Swine Fine Bucket

When our kids were old enough to have money of their own, I created a Swine Fine bucket. I painted a picture of a pig on the top of a small white plastic bucket and kept it on the kitchen counter. Whenever one of the boys behaved disrespectfully toward a family member or exhibited poor manners, I called out, "Swine fine!" The offender was required to deposit a designated amount of money (which I got to keep) into the bucket.

Don't talk about one child's problems to another child. And don't talk to your friends about any confidential matters your child shares with you.

Rule 8: Respect each other's space. Everyone needs a degree of privacy. We made a habit of always knocking before opening someone's closed door. All children need to have a sense of ownership and privacy. They need a place where they can daydream, try on clothes, experiment with makeup, practice shaving, and lie down quietly after a demanding day at school. Talk openly about giving one another space and respecting others' feelings.

When our oldest boys were teenagers, they shared a room. They had to learn to give each other privacy when needed. And since one of the boys could tolerate more mess than his orderly brother, they had to learn to think of each other's feelings and cut each other slack in this area as well.

When a family lives together in restricted space, it's important for everyone to be aware that sound travels and what a person does in one room affects others in a room nearby. When the boys turned on music in their room, they needed to recognize that I was down the hall, trying to finish a magazine article. It also meant that when my husband or I considered turning on the TV on a school night, we thought twice about it if a boy had not finished his homework or was trying to study for a test.

Rule 9: Respect each other's stuff. We all want our children to learn to respect the property of others and to share their belongings with others. To do this, they must have a sense of control over their belongings and respect the control someone else has over his or her things. At our house this meant if James had a friend over and they wanted to play with something that belonged to a big brother who wasn't home to give his permission, they had find something else to play with. It meant if Joel wanted to wear a sweater of John's, he had to ask John first. It also meant I had to respect their property as well.

When they were ready to establish their own family's House Rules, Grace and Mike went out to dinner without the kids. They decided to start by setting guidelines for their speech, since they were concerned about the negative tone that characterized a lot of the talk among the children and, increasingly, parent-child interaction. They admitted to each other that they had been using too many angry words and that they needed to set a good example for the children.

A few days later they had a family meeting and let the kids give their input into the House Rules. The children shared honestly how they felt about their home. Some of their comments were difficult for Grace to hear, but she knew that letting them express honest feelings was important to making the changes they needed.

In the week that followed, Mike agreed to try to get home a little earlier to help referee any breaches in their new House Rules, and Grace focused on establishing SOPs. She kept a notepad in her car and purse so she could jot ideas. She got into this in a big way!

The next weekend, at a second family meeting, Grace and Mike presented a united front and laid out their SOPs. There was a lot more resistance this time, especially about their decision to keep the TV off in the mornings. When their twelve-year-old said that was a stupid idea, his six-year-old sister yelled out, "Swine fine!" Despite a rocky start with a host of swine fines for griping, arguing, and name-calling, within a week there was a noticeable change in the mood and helpfulness of the kids. Mike continued to come home a little earlier from work—perhaps in part because home was becoming a more pleasant place.

Personal Reflection ✳

One of my pet peeves is "voice jail." It would indeed be sad if God had an automated answering system that said, "Hello. We're glad you called heaven. God is busy, but the first available angel will be with you momentarily. So we can better serve you, press 1 for daily scheduling help, 2 for parenting advice, 3 for marital counseling, and 4 for general Family Management support."

If this were the case, I would spend most of my life on hold because each day I have a lot of questions and frustrations. Thankfully such an answering service is the very opposite of reality. God tells us over and over again in the Bible that He is always near and cares intimately about every one of our questions and requests.

"Is any one of you in trouble? He should pray." (James 5:13)

Are you in trouble? What would you like to change about your daily routines and the atmosphere of your home? Take God at His Word. Tell Him about these things in prayer, and watch for His answers.

A mother stirs a little bit of herself into everything she cooks for her family.
Marjorie Holmes

....

You don't get over hating to cook, any more than you get over having big feet.
Peg Bracken

....

The person who decides what shall be the food and drink of a family, and the modes of its preparation, is the one who decides, to a greater or less extent, what shall be the health of that family.
Catharine E. Beecher &
Harriet Beecher Stowe,
The American Woman's Home,
1869

※

CHAPTER 8

Dinnertime Makeover

Winning the "What's for Dinner?" Battle

From the moment our boys were old enough to understand, Bill and I stressed the importance of being truthful and thankful. Unfortunately, my cooking has always put them in an awkward position. How can they honestly be thankful for dinner when they'd rather feed it to the dogs?

For years, I gave cooking my best shot. I pored over cookbooks and food magazines, attempted new recipes, and tried different techniques. I got into nutrition in a big way, banning white sugar and refined flour from our home. I made my own peanut butter, drove to a farm to buy honey straight from the hive, and baked all our bread before realizing that I'd gone overboard—when it was really my bread that should have. It would have made the perfect anchor.

For a number of reasons, my family's health in particular, I decided to accept the truth about myself and give up trying to be a culinary diva. I was out of my depth and had put my children in a compromising position about truthfully being thankful at dinnertime. We decided to work together as a family to make the evening meal a more positive experience.

First off, we voted that Bill should cook whenever possible. He's better at it than I am. That way the boys didn't have to worry about their turkey burgers turning into turkey jerky. I did most of the grocery shopping and table decorating. The boys became on-call sous-chefs and assistant table setters. We all worked together to plan meals. Each boy could add foods he liked and could honestly be thankful for—within reason.

Every Family Manager is going to have at least one department in which she feels like a failure. So, as the kids say, "Deal with it." The good news is that we can compensate for our weaknesses. Anyway, no executive manager ever claimed to be able to do all things equally

"Dining is and always was a great artistic opportunity."
—Frank Lloyd Wright

well, or even to do all things. Smart managers hire staff members who aren't replicas of themselves. If they're weak on details, they hire someone whose idea of fun is keeping track of the minutiae. If they know they're not good at systematizing and prioritizing, they hire people who are. The idea is to be smart—to use our skills, talents, and abilities to do what we do best and to delegate tasks that allow other people to do what they do best.

Food and teamwork go hand in hand, perhaps more naturally than any other area of Family Management. Eating and cooking together build bonds. Even the youngest child can, with encouragement, participate in family conversations around the dinner table *and* carry flatware or dishes to or from the table, wash carrots (even if they have to be rewashed), or help stir the corn bread batter.

But it's difficult for some women to delegate something they feel, for one reason or other, is "their job," especially something as integral to their family's welfare as food. This may sound like a small thing, but I felt indescribably free when I decided that it didn't make me less of a woman to let the men in my family take over the kitchen. And it didn't make me less of a mother to let someone else create my boys' birthday cakes. Each boy always wanted a special layered lemon cake— the same kind every year. I finally decided it was okay to order their cakes from the bakery. The boys were delighted, I was not crying over another cake I'd baked that looked like the Leaning Tower of Pisa, and Bill was happy that he never again had to bail me out by decorating over another cake disaster.

If delegating in the kitchen is difficult for you, or if you're the type of person who doesn't like your kitchen messy or has a hard time letting someone else do something you could do faster and better, consider the gift you are giving your children when you pass along to them on a daily basis the skills and knowledge you have about food. And consider how you and your husband could enjoy preparing dinner together while discussing the day's happenings—especially if you live in two different worlds most of the time.

What Goes into the Mix?

When you're thinking about managing the Food department of your family, discovering your family's "food DNA" is the place to start. Are you the experimental type? Is your family flexible enough to go along with those experiments occasionally? Do you like to try new recipes and new foods? Does your husband like to cook? Do you have older children who can cook? Does anyone in your family have special dietary needs?

No doubt you know the answer to most of these questions, and perhaps as you incorporate the Family Management concepts into your life, food is something you'll put on the back burner because your kitchen runs just fine, thank you very much. However, even if you're a whiz in the kitchen, you may count yourself among the many women who struggle with getting dinner on the table due to an overflowing daily schedule.

Good Family Management is about working smarter—and this applies to fixing dinner just as much as it applies to washing windows. Sure, good management of the Food department is about food preparation, cooking ahead, shortcut recipes, and the like, but it's also about being smart when it comes to the circumstances in your life. This means if you're the mother of three children under six, this is not the time to choose recipes that call for seventeen ingredients and take a minimum of two hours and lots of supervision to prepare. It means if you're a single mom with another full-time job outside the home and you have two teenage boys to feed, be smart. Buy in bulk, and buy foods your sons can fix themselves.

Planning Menus Your Whole Family Will Love

Many mothers complain that their children are picky eaters. I feel their pain, because my boys were always finicky about food. I tend to look at this as sort of a chicken-and-egg thing. Maybe they were born that way. Or maybe my cooking affected them more adversely than I thought. Or maybe most young children are conservative creatures of habit and thereby labeled finicky eaters. Whatever the reason, I found that it helped to involve everybody in menu planning. This is good to do periodically even if you're not dealing with picky eaters. Get some paper and a pencil to take notes, then have everybody call out their favorite foods, what they'd like to eat that you haven't fixed for a while, or maybe something you've never served but a child enjoyed at a friend's house. You can organize your brainstorming list by meal—breakfast, lunch, dinner—or by category—fruit, vegetable, meat, etc. Or you can simply list everything and organize it later.

Remind everybody of the basic ground rules of brainstorming before you start: (1) There are no stupid or wrong ideas.

Every food mentioned goes on the list. (2) No critical commenting on another person's suggestions is allowed. No "aarghs" when things like quiche or green beans are mentioned. (3) As with any other meeting, only one person talks at a time.

> "In general my children refuse to eat anything that hasn't danced on TV."
> —Erma Bombeck

Once the meeting is over, all you have to do is organize the foods into reasonable menus. If family members mention foods that are unavailable, unhealthy, or totally outside the realm of your ability to afford or prepare, you can discuss that later. Just get started now with what works.

Family Manager Coach Ramsey Johansson shared the story of how one of her clients started working smarter and was able to take control of meals for her family of six. Here is Ramsey's account of a woman named Laura.

Laura's Story

Laura, a pastor's wife, was constantly on the move, spending a lot of time and energy juggling schedules and logistics. She worked full-time at a title company, taught women's Bible study and marriage classes at her church, and shuttled her four children to and from three schools and extracurricular activities.

All this running around left Laura spent, and mealtimes suffered. Breakfast was often served—or shoved—in the car.

A Good Option for Busy Moms

Judie Byrd is founder of the Culinary School of Fort Worth and a close, longtime friend. She loves to teach people to cook— although she never made much progress with me. Judie and I were neighbors when our children were young, and we had lots of laughs over my kitchen catastrophes.

In 2003, Judie launched Super Suppers, and I'd like to think I was at least part of her inspiration. She started her entrée assembly stores to meet the needs of busy parents who want to create quality family time around the dinner table— but don't have the extra time and energy (or, in my case, the skill) to cook meals from scratch. I wish she had thought of this when my kids were young!

The children ate school cafeteria lunches every day. Dinner was usually an afterthought—and most often fast food. She and her family members were frustrated by the lack of healthy, fresh, home-cooked food in their diets, and Laura was frustrated by the lack of time to plan, shop, and cook. She dreaded evenings, not knowing what she'd serve for dinner.

Laura wanted to change her ways, and her health now required it as she was under a doctor's care for high blood pressure.

Laura ended up developing her own system for meal planning. She writes each meal on a Post-it note and then arranges the notes on her calendar for the week. If the scheduled meal doesn't work on its designated day, she simply moves the Post-it notes around. She keeps the meal calendar in a central location, and each family member can see at a glance what's being served.

"Where's the cook? Is supper ready, the house trimmed, rushes strewed, cobwebs swept?"
—*William Shakespeare*

"Everyone loves my schedule," Laura said. "Even when I have to switch the foods around because I come home later than expected, I have so many things on hand that I have become the 'Whip-Up-Something-Delicious-in-Minutes Queen.' Even my husband is saying, 'So, where'd you get this recipe?' I reply, 'I didn't—I made it up as I went!'"

Food for Body and Soul

Making the most of mealtimes requires more than planning healthy meals in advance, however. There's something about sitting down and eating together—especially when everybody has had a hand, no matter how small, in getting the meal on the table—that promotes family bonding. And after a hard day, it's wonderful to eat dinner with people you love. Since I don't add much to the quality of the food at my home outside of a few dishes I've mastered, I see my most important role as initiating good conversation that brings out the best of the diners, whether they're my own family or guests we've invited to share our meal.

Dinnertime is about more than food. Studies published by the University of Minnesota and the University of North Carolina report that kids who grew up in households where parents were present at crucial times—especially during meals—were better adjusted than other children. An American Psychological Association study reported that well-adjusted teenagers—those with better relationships with their peers, more academic motivation, and fewer, if any, problems with drugs and alcohol—ate dinner with their families an average of five days a week. If your schedule has squeezed out time around the table, consider these simple steps to reclaim family dinnertime at your house.

1. Make a decision to eat together certain nights each week— and do it with rare exceptions allowed. Your kids might

Makeover Strategies for Healthy Family Dinners

PROBLEM
You frequently don't decide what your family will have for dinner until late in the afternoon. If you're lucky, you can find something to thaw in the microwave. If not, you head to the closest fast-food outlet again.

SOLUTION
Designate a specific time each week to plan your family's meals and to do your grocery shopping. Once you've planned the menus, jot them on a calendar or another central spot so you can quickly refer to the list throughout the week.

PROBLEM
You are constantly struggling to come up with ideas for dinners your family will actually eat.

SOLUTION
Constantly be on the lookout for simple, nutritious recipes requiring few ingredients. Include your family in the process by asking them for meal ideas. As you plan your meals for the week ahead, allow each family member to pick one dinner menu.

PROBLEM
You often need to stop by the grocery store on your way home from work to pick up just one or two items.

SOLUTION
Create or download a grocery list that you can use to check off items you need throughout the week. Stock your pantry with staples like low-fat cream soups and chicken broth so you can more easily throw together a meal on a particularly harried evening or when unexpected guests stop by at dinnertime.

GOAL: *Plan and prepare healthy meals and eat together as a family several evenings each week.*

PROBLEM

Planning a variety of dinners for every night of the week has become overwhelming.

SOLUTION

Launch a designated pasta night or taco night each week. Both meals appeal to everyone in the family, and the ingredients and preparation are simple. And if every Wednesday is taco night, that's one less meal to worry about when planning your meals for that week.

PROBLEM

The hour before dinner is always hectic as you prepare dinner, set the table, and get after-school snacks for your kids.

SOLUTION

Many tasks associated with dinner preparation and cleanup—from setting the table to making individual salads—are perfect jobs for kids of any age. By requiring them to help out, you're teaching them important life skills. Anyway, it's not good for them to grow up believing that it's Mom's responsibility to do everything.

PROBLEM

When you're in the frozen foods section of your grocery store, you often consider buying some frozen ready-to-serve dinners to have on hand for busy days. However, you've noticed they're pricey and would break your food budget.

SOLUTION

Set aside a day to prepare meals calling for the same meat or poultry (such as chicken enchiladas, potpie, and soup). Begin by gathering all the ingredients and supplies. As you stew the chicken breasts, prepare the other ingredients. Before you know it, you'll have several separate meals ready for your freezer.

protest at first, and you may have to adjust your schedule. But remember, you're building for the future.

2. Beware of the "whining hour." If you have small children, have some light, healthy snacks to tide them over until dinnertime. If you work outside the home, try to arrange your dinner prep time so you don't have to start cooking the moment you walk in the door at the end of the day. Devote the first fifteen or twenty minutes exclusively to your child, whether to read a story, check homework, or just cuddle.

3. Cook smart. Develop a repertoire of easy meals, and always keep the ingredients on hand. Don't let complicated recipes and menus limit the time your family can sit around the dinner table and talk about the day. It's more important to eat together than to eat elaborate meals.

4. Predetermine and post menus. With tight schedules and parent burnout at the end of the day, the last thing you need is disorder and dissension over what to fix for dinner.

5. Assign everyone a meal-related job. Cooking and working cooperatively with other family members teaches kids responsibility and important skills they'll use the rest of their lives. Even young children can learn early that they're part of the family team. A three-year-old can help set the table, tear lettuce, wash vegetables, or just play with cooking "toys" while parents and older siblings prepare dinner.

6. Clean up as you go. When cooking, immediately return

used ingredients to where they belong and toss all wrappers and scraps. Always fill your sink with warm water and soap while cooking. Soak pots, pans, and utensils while you're eating for easier cleanup later.

7. Start and finish your meal together. Make sure everyone who is at home is seated at the beginning of the meal. And even though kids may complain, you're teaching good manners when you have them remain at the table until everyone is excused.

8. Disconnect with the outside world and connect with your family. Turn off the television and mute telephones, cell phones, PDAs, and computers. Break the "I have to see who needs me" habit. Your family needs you now.

9. Promote positive conversation. Ban critical words and arguing at the table. Avoid disciplinary discussions that could be handled at another time. Dinner is not the time to discuss problems at school.

10. Get quality conversations started by asking questions like, "What interesting thing happened today?" or "What made you feel happy today?" If it's hard to spark a conversation, try taking turns going around the table and having each family member tell about something new they learned that day. Or, depending on the age of your child, use one the following questions to start a discussion:

- What is something you've always wanted to learn to do?

- If you could be president of the United States for one day, what would you do?

- Where did you notice God at work today?

- If you could eat dinner with three people from history, whom would you choose?

- If you could travel anyplace in the world this summer, where would you go and what would you do?

Claire's Story

Claire, like Laura, was frustrated when it came to feeding her family. She wanted her family of five to eat dinner together, enjoying good food and fun conversation around the table at the end of the day. But it wasn't happening—neither the good food nor the fun. Claire was discouraged because when she prepared what she considered a good dinner, the kids would gripe and complain about what they didn't like and ask for something else. Add in her kids' afternoon activities and her husband's unpredictable schedule, and most of us can at least sympathize with why she finally just gave up trying to eat dinner as a family. But she knew this wasn't the right thing to do.

I met with Claire and her husband, Josh, to discuss how they could work together to bring back family dinnertime. They knew this would be best for their kids, so they made a commitment to do whatever they could to make it happen. Josh agreed to try to get home from work in time to help with dinner preparation on as many nights as possible. Claire said she would be more disciplined about keeping the needed ingredients on hand for meals and not wait until the last minute to plan and prepare dinner. They both would work on table manners and conversation guidelines, and come up with consequences for those who did not cooperate.

The actions they decided to take were fairly simple, but each one helped in working toward their goal. I created the chart on page 142 to show Claire and Josh how small actions can have big repercussions. For example, when they achieved all six elements in the top row of the chart, it was highly likely they would enjoy dinnertime as a family and strengthen relationships. But if they failed to live up to just one of the elements in that top row, the results would be diminished. While meeting at least some of these elements paid off, the best results came when they met all of them.

"The most remarkable thing about my mother is that for thirty years she served the family nothing but leftovers. The original meal has never been found."

—*Calvin Trillin*

Food for Thought

If you effectively manage the Food department, a lot of things will run more smoothly. You eliminate time-robbing trips to the store and save money by cutting back on fast food because you need food fast. When meals are planned in advance, with

Commitment Make eating dinner together a family priority. Keep long-term benefits in mind.	Teamwork Family member's help with some part of dinner prep or cleanup.	Table Rules Set guidelines to promote courtesy and kindness.	Resources Plan easy menus. Keep necessary ingredients on hand.	Time Management Practice advance work. Don't overschedule afternoons.	Conversation Initiate positive and interesting discussions.	Result Realize that simple choices really do make a difference.
✓	✓	✓	✓	✓	✓	Enjoy dinnertime together; strengthen relationships
.....	✓	✓	✓	✓	✓	Occasionally eat dinner together, if it's convenient
✓	.....	✓	✓	✓	✓	Feel resentful, unappreciated
✓	✓	.....	✓	✓	✓	Bickering, nagging, unpleasant experience likely
✓	✓	✓	.....	✓	✓	Frustration, guilt; waste time and money
✓	✓	✓	✓	.....	✓	Few dinners eaten together; too much fast food
✓	✓	✓	✓	✓	.....	Lost opportunities for growth and encouragement

all the food and ingredients on hand, everyone tends to feel calmer. Mornings are much less stressful because you have breakfast foods on hand. When your husband calls home on the spur of the moment to tell you that he's bringing a friend home for dinner in thirty minutes, you can simply shift into emergency-guest mode and pull out the hors d'oeuvres—the ones you keep hidden from your children for such a time as this. The transition from afternoon to evening in your home will be less stressful if you're managing food well.

Personal Reflection

Food has a lot to do with the culture of our homes. How we talk about food, how we act around it, as well as what we serve and when and under what circumstances we eat, speak volumes about our family and give our children positive attitudes for life.

Think about how you would describe your family based on your meal routines. What attitudes about food and family are your children learning?

"Go to the ant, you sluggard; consider its ways and be wise! It has no commander, no overseer or ruler, yet it stores its provisions in summer and gathers its food at harvest." (Proverbs 6:6-8)

Are there ways you want to be a better manager of this important part of your job and your family's life? What's one step you can take today to move in that direction?

66 **How many things I can do without!** 99

Socrates

....

66 **There is a time for everything . . . a time to keep and a time to throw away.** 99

Ecclesiastes 3:1, 6

....

66 **We shape our buildings, then our buildings shape us.** 99

Winston Churchill

✳

CHAPTER 9

Clutter Makeover

.... *Fast Track to an Organized Home*

Transforming a house into a home is the Family Manager's most rewarding task. One way we shape our homes is by shouldering the responsibility for what shape it's in, from the physical structure itself to everything that's in it and around it. For starters, we're talking about cleaning, storing, maintaining, organizing, and/or enhancing the house, yard, furniture, accessories, decor, appliances, tools, electronic equipment, books, documents, clothing, toys, and sports equipment. No small job, as you well know.

But as Family Managers, we're also the primary shapers of the people who live within a house's walls. Home is so much more than the place where we eat, sleep, play, and recuperate from the stresses of the day. It's where we nourish and nurture our children, bandage their boo-boos, and guide their growth. Home is where the heart is because it's the place where meaningful memories are made.

The climate of our homes greatly affects the development, or *shaping*, of the people who live there. Clutter and lack of organization are like storm clouds in the home. They bring floods of frustration and interfere with our comfort and security. No matter what the size of a home, too much stuff and misused storage spaces can make any mom a meanie, and when Mom's not happy, it's hard for anyone to be happy.

Ideally, home reflects and facilitates who we are and who we are becoming—"we" being our family. The closets in my house would never be photographed for a magazine. I've concluded that having cover-story-worthy storage spaces is just not that important. Knowing what we have, being able to find what we need when we need it, and being able to get to it without a cherry picker are.

"What is more agreeable than one's home?"

—Cicero

When it comes to having organized closets and cupboards, my friend Pam gets the prize. Pam's definition of an orderly closet is one in which blouses, pants, skirts, and dresses all face the same direction on the same kind of hanger and are categorized by color. Her closets are pleasing to look at because the clothes are hung according to length.

I like order, but it doesn't come naturally for me. Herculean efforts would be required for my closets to be as neat as Pam's. But whether it's my closet or the bathroom cabinets, I'm always searching for ways to bring more order to my home.

I like opening a closet or cabinet without fear of what I might find there—or what I won't.

Whoever we are, we're wise to use whatever storage space we have prudently. We'll waste less time looking for things we need, and we'll spend less money because we know what we have and won't buy duplicates (I hate it when I do that!). When Jennie got a household makeover, she was in the midst of dealing with this very challenge.

Jennie's Story

On most fronts, Jennie's home was running pretty well. After several years at home, she had recently gone back to teaching school, so her time was compressed. Her home had a very large closet—about eight feet square, so it was more like a small room—that she had claimed for seasonal decorations, wrapping supplies, and miscellaneous items. It was a big selling point when her family bought the house. The problem was that she hadn't kept up with the contents of the closet, and it had become almost impossible to step through the door. The space was crammed with decorations, gift wrap, gifts, papers, old clothes, and boxes and crates of this and that. Though taming this beast was high on her to-do list, she hadn't gotten to it yet. In the meantime, she wasted precious minutes clearing a pathway and digging through messy piles to locate needed items, often coming up empty handed.

Family Manager Coach Teri Fulton helped Jennie transform

this space from frustrating to functional. Together they pulled everything out of the closet and then created "departments" where items would be placed when they were put back in. Boxes of photographs were labeled and put on shelves against one wall. When Jennie found a few minutes to work on photo albums, she knew where to find the photos she needed. Decorations were stored on another wall, segregated by holiday. A gift-wrap center was set up on another wall. A large Peg-Board (easy to install) with hooks came in handy for ribbons, gift bags, and scissors. In the process of excavating the closet, they uncovered numerous rolls of wrapping paper, as well as all those birthday party gifts and end-of-the-year teacher gifts Jennie had been looking for. Buying ahead can be a huge time-saver, but it is a complete waste if you can't find items when you need them. Jennie's story is a good clutter lesson for all of us.

But what do you do if you don't have a giant closet like Jennie's? I once worked with a family who decided to add on to their home to accommodate all their stuff. I thought to myself, *Wow! Nice if you have that option, but knocking out a wall to create a new closet every time an old one is filled is not an option for most of us.* We have to find other ways to maximize our space, organize our belongings, and provide the breathing space we need to make our homes run efficiently.

Family Manager Coach Heather Radzinski worked with a young family of four who lived in an older home that had loads of charm but very little storage space. The house had a basement with storage potential, a few small closets, and a kitchen with limited cabinets and drawers. Heather had to discover ways some of the unused space in their home could be turned into efficient storage.

The couple's two young girls shared a bedroom, so Heather added a rod doubler in their closest to increase hanging space for pants and skirts. She maximized the space underneath their beds with under-bed storage boxes for their personal belongings. She also used under-bed stor-

> "Think of what you can do with what there is."
>
> —*Ernest Hemingway*

age boxes in the parents' bedroom, as well as over-the-door shoe organizers to maximize space behind doors.

She added hooks underneath kitchen cabinets to hang coffee cups and used various sizes of labeled plastic bins to store miscellaneous items on shelves in the basement. These organizing supplies were not fancy or expensive, but they made the most of unused areas and helped the family enjoy their home.

Don't Be Your Own Worst Enemy

Of course, we can't blame all our clutter management woes on lack of space or time. We create some of them ourselves. In fact, we can sabotage our goals quickly by falling prey to procrastination. We may truly want our homes to be clutter free so that all family members feel they are entering an orderly, pleasant oasis when they return home. At the same time, the thought of getting serious about finding new storage areas and getting rid of stuff may weigh us down so much that we readily abandon our goal in favor of planting bulbs around the oak tree in our front yard.

Melinda had been procrastinating about cleaning out the spare bedroom for months. A busy loan officer in Michigan, Melinda had moved into a starter home with her husband, David, just days after their wedding the year before. They'd never really had time to fix up the extra room. Since they didn't have a basement, the room quickly became a catchall. It irritated Melinda a bit, and she constantly told David they should set aside a Saturday to clean it.

The trouble was, it was easy to keep procrastinating because they could always keep the door to this room shut. You know how it is . . . out of sight, out of mind. Then one day her in-laws, who live several states away and had never seen their son's home, called to say they would be passing through in a couple of weeks and would love to spend a few days with them.

Melinda flipped into panic mode and called David. They got serious about the project fast and decided to get it done the following Saturday. They got out all the cleaners, rags, buckets, vacuum, and other supplies the night before. They also wrote down a detailed list of each step they wanted to accomplish the following day. Melinda even jotted a line next to

Overlooked Storage Space

Walk from room to room in your home and look for new storage space you hadn't thought of before. Use these ideas to spur your thinking.

- Put a towel rack on the back of your linen closet door to hold tablecloths and seasonal runners.
- Think "up high." Build a high-border shelf around the perimeter of a room to store/display decorative items such as baskets, decorative dishes, trophies, or collectible dolls.
- Invest in some small rolling carts, which fit underneath desks or in closets. They work well for storing and easily accessing art supplies and sewing machines and materials.
- Don't overlook those "behind" places. Store your dining room table leaves behind the china closet or breakfront. A fold-up easel may hang on the wall behind a child's closet door.
- Add a to-the-floor dust ruffle to the bottom of a baby crib for hidden floor storage.
- Put an over-the-door shoe organizer on the back of a door to store office supplies, hair products and accessories, or craft supplies.

each step so she'd have the pleasure of checking it off when it was finished!

After going to bed earlier than usual the night before, they got up and ate a light breakfast. David looked out at the sunny March morning and whined a bit about not getting to play golf that day. Melinda suggested they go for a quick walk while the street was still quiet. They did, and they were surprised to find that they actually felt invigorated and anxious to start on the room when they returned.

They had decided they would first organize and pack away all the clutter—unused wedding gifts, old textbooks, miscellaneous items from their separate apartments—that they'd been shoving into the room since their wedding. David placed a CD player and a stack of their favorite CDs next to the bedroom door. Melinda laughed as she took a mop and began dancing around the room with it. As she finished her shimmying act, David ran to his truck to pull out the dozen plastic storage bins they'd bought to organize all the clutter.

Before long, they had two sets of boxes. One was filled with items to be given away or pitched, the other with items for the attic. After carrying boxes up to the attic, David called for a break. They grabbed some fruit and water and took a few minutes' rest on their front porch. They confess that they scrambled back inside when they saw a talkative neighbor who lived down the block leave her house to walk her dog. They wanted to stay focused on the task until they finished!

They still had to dust mop the room, vacuum the floor, wash the windows, and put linens on the bed. Referring often to their list, the couple worked quickly. Melinda was amazed. The job she'd been dreading almost since the day they'd moved in was finished—and now she had a night out with David to look forward to. After all, they'd agreed it was only appropriate that they reward themselves with dinner at their favorite Mexican restaurant.

Declutter in a Day

Not all stories of procrastinating about clutter are as quickly solvable as David and Melinda's. After all, they didn't have children to take into consideration. But even if your schedule is more complex, it's worth farming out the kids to Grandma or a friend to schedule a serious decluttering day.

If you are ready to take a stand against clutter in your home—whether in one room or your whole house, a one-day clutter sweep will help immensely. The following ten-step plan will make the process much easier:

1. Arrange your schedule to do clutter battle on one day. This way you'll save on start-up/knock-down time; you'll be more serious and do a more thorough job. As you see the results, you'll gain the momentum you need to keep going.

2. Schedule the Salvation Army or another charity to come to your house soon after your decluttering day. This gives you a deadline.

3. Dress so you can put all your energy into the job. Wear comfortable clothes and tennis shoes.

4. Go into battle prepared. You'll need several types of containers: three boxes labeled "Give Away," "Garage Sale," and "Store"; plastic storage bins (the see-through kind are best); and a large plastic garbage bag for every room. If you think you'll be distracted by things you don't know what to do with, put them in a box too. Label the box "Questionable" and give yourself a deadline for deciding where those difficult items will end up. Also have a small box to collect safety pins and buttons, a shoe-size box for random photos you find, and another box or a piggy bank for coins.

5. Start with the most cluttered room in your house. Work your way methodically around the room. Remove clutter from shelves, bookcases, drawers, tabletops, floors, and walls.

6. Toss or give away as much as possible. Be ruthless with things like gift boxes, grocery sacks, old magazines and catalogs, and craft materials you saved but haven't used. Weed out games.

7. Broken objects are also clutter—they're not useful and not decorative. (The one exception: antiques, which can often be restored for less than the cost of a new piece.) Either get them fixed or give them away to a charity that repairs donated items.

8. Use strict criteria in your closet. Get rid of anything permanently stained or badly worn. Clothes you haven't put on in the last three years and trendy items that aren't well made should also go.

9. Don't allow nonemergencies to interrupt your clutter-clearing time. Eliminate all distractions. Turn on your answering machine, turn off the TV, and put on some peppy music. When you find the umbrella your friend left at your house three months ago, don't call her now to tell her about it. Or the book that's been missing—don't take a break now to crack it open.

10. If it's hard for you to toss things, arrange for a family member or friend—someone who knows you're serious about clamping down on clutter—to help you. Or visit www. familymanager.com to find out if there's a Family Manager Coach in your area who can help.

Prescription for Procrastination

If you'd like to tackle the clutter in your home but just aren't motivated or able to devote a full day to declutter yet, don't give up. By taking the following small steps, you'll begin to address the problem.

Set deadlines. Deadlines are the best guarantee a job will be done. Jot down on your calendar the time or day you want to have a task completed. If need be, ask a friend or family member to hold you accountable.

Make appointments to get things done. Don't wait for time to free up. If you have a big project to accomplish, schedule work appointments with yourself in thirty-minute or one-hour blocks. Be serious about this time like you would any other appointment. Before you know it, you'll have the project licked.

Be prepared. The projects you have the tools or resources for will be finished before the ones you're not prepared for. For example, if you schedule time to organize a closet, have on hand various sizes of organizing bins, self-sealing plastic bags, garbage bags, and boxes for giveaway items.

Whether clutter is a big or little problem for you, when you start winning the battle against it, you'll notice how good it feels—how much easier your life is without it. After I worked with Katie, she told me she felt as if she had a new lease on life and every step toward conquering the clutter in her home was more than worthwhile.

Katie's Story

Katie and I got to know each other over coffee at the clean end of her kitchen table. She said she felt as if she'd lost control—of her kitchen, laundry room, and closets.

When her twin daughters left for college, Katie and her husband decided to downsize from a large home to one that would be easier to maintain. With just the two of them and their son living at home, they didn't need as much living space. But they still needed storage space, and their new house had much less than their old one. This precipitated a number of issues that affected their ability to enjoy their home and belongings. "It's hard to count your blessings when you can't find them!" she said.

As Katie and I walked through her home to assess how we could make it a fun and functional place, two problems stood out immediately. First, clutter was taking over in almost every room. When they moved out of their old home, they did not give away or throw away things they didn't use or want. These items cluttered the closets, cupboards, and corners of rooms in their new home. And like many families, they continued to accumulate more things, which intensified the problem.

Another issue was misused storage space. The laundry room was crammed with household items as well as dirty and clean clothes. As for the bedrooms, Katie had taken over three closets in different rooms, each one disorganized and filled with clothes she didn't wear often, if at all. She told me that getting dressed in the morning was like a circus act as

"Go home, and take care of what you have. Provide places for all your things."
—Mother Ann Lee, Shaker founder

she wrapped herself in a towel and ran from room to room, searching for matching tops, bottoms, and accessories. We laughed as she described her antics, but I knew it wasn't so funny every morning when she was trying to get dressed.

When we looked in her kitchen cupboards, various sizes of repurposed plastic tubs and tops tumbled out. Even her refrigerator and freezer had been taken over by clutter. The fridge was filled with old food and duplicates. Her freezer shelves were laden with UFOs—unidentified frozen objects, unmarked and wrapped in foil.

After our walk-through, we worked on a plan to get some key areas under control quickly. We also discussed how to get her husband and son to work with her to control the clutter and make it a place they all enjoyed.

For the next two days, we worked like Energizer bunnies. See-through plastic bins came to the rescue in the laundry room, which doubled as a storage room for tools and as a depository for things that didn't have a home. Shelves on one wall held a little bit of everything. We removed everything from the shelves and started sorting— tossing old and broken items as we went. Then we piled the like items together in storage bins and put them neatly on the shelves after labeling each bin. This way, if family members needed a certain kind of tape, glue, lightbulb, or screwdriver, they would know exactly where to find it—and where to return supplies.

"Order is the shape upon which beauty depends."

—Pearl Buck

We added a few more simple conveniences to make the laundry room more usable. We attached a small plastic container with suction cups to the side of the dryer, perfect for holding guitar picks, coins, and small toys rescued from pockets. We placed a medium-size bin on top of the dryer as the designated home for orphan socks. We also added a small trash can nearby, ready for dryer lint and other items that can't be recycled.

Next we tackled Katie's closets. We started by clearing out her main closet to get an idea of everything she owned and the amount of existing storage space. We sorted through her clothes, separating winter and fall items from spring and summer items. We put clothes that no longer fit or just weren't flattering in a box destined for the Salvation Army thrift store.

We packed away out-of-season items and placed them on top shelves, away from valuable everyday space. We gathered extra linens and blankets and packed them in storage boxes that fit under beds, taking advantage of unused space and clearing closet space for more in-demand items. When we hung clothes back in her closet, we organized them by type—blouses, pants, skirts, jackets, dresses—and then by color. We also placed her

For every underused item that is taking up space in your house, ask these questions:

- When is the last time it was used? worn? played with?
- Does it deserve space in our home?
- What will I do with it? Fix it, sell it, store it, toss it, or donate it?

most frequently worn items front and center so the things she needed most often would be most accessible.

Finally, we moved to the kitchen and began purging her refrigerator. If she was unsure of the age of a food, drink, or condiment, we tossed it. When we found duplicates, such as two bottles of ketchup, we combined the contents when possible or threw away the older one.

The freezer needed attention too. We searched for expiration dates, unwrapped the unknown items, and threw out old food. When she was able to see into the depths of her freezer, Katie had a new appreciation for see-through, labeled containers. If you can't see what's inside, you're less likely to know what's hiding in there and less likely to use the food.

As for her kitchen cabinets, we only had time to tackle one of them. We tossed the storage containers that were old or had no lids and replaced them with stackable, disposable containers, which took up much less space than the jumbled mess she'd been struggling with.

Two days was not enough time to get her entire house in order, but Katie already felt greatly relieved by the progress we'd made. She also had a plan to get the rest of her home under control and strategies to keep it in order.

Defeating clutter and getting the storage areas in your home under control are not done in a day. In fact, they're never *done*. Controlling clutter and keeping your belongings organized are ongoing processes. As was the case for Bonnie and Tracy, profiled in chapter 4, few women have large blocks of time to work through their house in one fell swoop.

If you can't see a free day in the next few years, try getting into the "Power of Ten" mind-set. You'd be surprised how much you can accomplish in ten minutes and how many "free" ten-minute snippets of time you can grab here and there.

Granted, you won't finish tasks like cleaning out all your closets or unloading the basement of five years' worth of magazines with articles about how to get organized, but you'll make progress a little bit at a time—and eventually get the job done.

Here's a sample list of tasks you can do in ten minutes:

- Clear off a catchall surface—like part of a countertop, a coffee table, or the top of the dryer.

- Grab a trash bag and clean out odds and ends from your freezer.

- Throw out old foods from refrigerator crisper drawers and wipe the drawers clean. (Line drawers with paper towels so next time you can just toss the dirty paper towel and replace it with a clean one.)

- Purge a shelf or two in your pantry of food that has outlived its suggested shelf life.

- Chip away at a larger project you've been putting off, such as cleaning out kitchen cabinets and drawers. Work for ten

Makeover Strategies for Clutter Control

PROBLEM

You put away and throw away clutter on your weekly marathon cleaning day, yet the next day, your house is once again littered with toys, laundry, and papers.

SOLUTION

Sometime after dinner, have a decluttering dash. Set a timer for seven to ten minutes. Put on some favorite energizing music and play "beat the clock." Have everyone work at picking up misplaced items and returning them to where they belong before the buzzer sounds.

PROBLEM

Everyone in your family is a packrat.

SOLUTION

Have a clutter-purging contest once a month. Put medium-size boxes, one for each family member, in a central location. (Items to be given away go here.) Give each family member a plastic garbage bag and spend thirty minutes rounding up items to give or throw away. The person who gathers the most gets to pick where to eat out as a reward.

PROBLEM

You're not sure how and where to store things for maximum efficiency.

SOLUTION

Store items as close as possible to the place they are used most often. If you only iron when you're touching up something to wear immediately, keep your iron and ironing board in your closet, not the laundry room. Decide which cabinets and drawers are most easily accessible in your kitchen. Store the items you use most there.

GOAL: *Take control over the clutter that is multiplying throughout your home.*

PROBLEM
Everyone is in the habit of leaving things out when they're through with them.

SOLUTION
Make your family motto "Put it up, not down." Start encouraging family members to return everything they get out where it belongs. Designate a fine for people who leave items in places they don't belong. Kids love this rule because they can make money when they catch Mom or Dad leaving things out.

PROBLEM
You never seem to have time to declutter and organize your storage areas.

SOLUTION
Set a goal to finish one closet, cupboard, or storage area each week until you've worked your way through the house. During busy weeks, tackle something small like a medicine cabinet or a shelf in your linen closet so you won't lose momentum.

PROBLEM
Despite occasional attempts to clean it, you have a closet in your family room that has become a catchall area for art supplies, holiday decorations, and office supplies.

SOLUTION
Accept that you won't have the time or inclination to keep every space in your home immaculate. Still it is worth making storage spaces functional. If you can't find what you need in that closet, set aside time to remove everything and reorganize the contents in appropriately sized storage boxes or cabinets.

minutes on one cabinet or drawer at a time, and watch your dream of having tidy, clean storage spaces materialize before your very eyes.

- Dust part of your bedroom, or at least get the dust bunnies under the bed, and spot-clean picture frames.

- Straighten a shelf or two in the linen closet.

- Walk through your house with a plastic garbage bag and see how much clutter you can gather. Toss out things like expired coupons, old catalogs and magazines, single or worn-out socks (save a few for cleaning), extra grocery bags (keep only four or five on hand), items that are beyond-hope broken, games with missing pieces, and the like. Do this the night before garbage pickup so you won't be tempted to retrieve anything.

Write your own list of ten-minute tasks, and post it in a central location. Recruit family members to practice the Power of Ten. Every time you "catch" someone using free minutes to get something done, offer words of praise or give a weekly reward to the person who accrues the most segments. Before you know it, all those minutes used productively here and there will free up a large block of time you can use for rest and recreation—well-deserved rewards.

On the days when you get tired of fighting clutter, remem-

ber the benefits: It helps you and your family live more efficiently and makes your home a more pleasant place for all.

Personal Reflection ✳

A home can become filled with clutter for many reasons, some
of which we cannot control. Maybe your mother-in-law moved in
with your family, and it's going to take time to sort through the
belongings she collected over many years. Some forms of clutter, however, we can control.

Have you ever stopped to consider why you keep accumulat-
ing more "stuff"? Do your children feel that they need to have the
latest fads or fashions? Do you compulsively buy things because
they're on sale? Do you watch TV shopping programs and order
items that you hope will make you lose weight, look younger,
or make you happier? When we buy things because we think
they are a "must," we have a problem. This is a sure sign that
we are seeking our identity from things that won't ever bring us
satisfaction.

All of us need to differentiate between our needs and wants.
Take some time to think about why clutter has become an issue
in your home.

> "I have learned the secret of being content in any and every
> situation, whether well fed or hungry, whether living in plenty
> or in want. I can do everything through him who gives me
> strength." (Philippians 4:12-13)

> **Start by doing what's necessary, then what's possible, and suddenly you are doing the impossible.**
> Saint Francis of Assisi

....

> **He that won't be counseled can't be helped.**
> Benjamin Franklin

....

> **I waited patiently for the LORD; he turned to me and heard my cry. He lifted me out of the slimy pit, out of the mud and mire; he set my feet on a rock and gave me a firm place to stand.**
> Psalm 40:1–2

※

CHAPTER 10

Time Management Makeover

The Courage to Call for Help

When Larry and Rachael married nearly fifteen years ago, they eagerly anticipated building a home and family together. They never dreamed that their lives would become so stressful that Rachael would secretly enter a Life Makeover contest. But out of desperation, she did. And she won.

As the designated Family Management expert for the contest, I was dispatched to their home in Ohio. Larry was puttering in their yard when I arrived. I introduced myself and was taken aback by his hostile tone—not to mention his strange question: "Which one are you?"

Undeterred, I cheerfully told him I was a family management expert and had been sent to work with his family by the sponsor of the makeover contest.

Leaning over his rake, he looked me squarely in the eyes. I wasn't sure whether he wanted to run me off his property or shoot me on the spot. Finally, he said, "Look, my wife and I don't need another expert telling us how to whip our lives into shape." Then he explained that the sponsor had already sent over a fitness trainer, a financial expert, and a meditation specialist as part of their makeover prize.

No wonder Larry was frustrated. The fitness expert told him and Rachael that they needed to work out every morning, despite the fact that they struggled to get their kids to school before the tardy bell rang. The next expert had created a detailed financial plan—a little premature and daunting for a couple who didn't even know where to find bills that were due the following week. And they didn't know what to make of their sessions with the meditation expert.

The couple felt as if they were already drowning in stress, and now they were weighed down even more by what these experts told them to do. What they needed first and foremost was help in bringing order to their domestic chaos and peace to their frazzled family.

I spent two days at their disorderly home. I listened as they voiced frustrations and told me about the dreams for their family that had gotten lost in the confusion five children can add to life. I identified their key issues and suggested some stress-relieving strategies.

Many of the solutions we discussed centered on making the best use of their time—not only to accomplish their work but to bring fun back into their home. At the end of our second day together, Rachael held their toddler and tearfully waved good-bye to me from their door. Larry walked me to the car and gave me a big hug before I got in. I could tell he was glad he hadn't shot me.

Here's another contest winner's story I think you'll relate to. Vicki wrote this on the entry form of a Family Makeover contest:

We are in desperate need of some help. I think my husband is at his wit's end with the chaos he has to come home to every evening. And I shudder to think what this is setting our children up for when they have their own homes.

We feel that if you pick us, our family life will change dramatically. No longer will we run out of the house mad at each other because we were screaming 'hurry up,' or 'I can't find my ____.' We will have the peace of mind that comes with knowing that everything has a place and there is a place for everything. We will be able to get places on time, with everything we need.

Most important, I hope that once Kathy Peel has finished our family makeover, our home will become a haven for my husband and kids to come home to after a long day

> "Time is the scarcest resource, and unless it is managed, nothing else can be managed."
> —Peter Drucker

of work and school. There is enough stress out there in the world. Home should be someplace you can come home, take your shoes off (and put them in their designated place!), and breathe a sigh of relief.

It took a lot of courage for Vicki to write this description of her home, but she was desperate. And as it happened, she won the contest.

Vicki's Story

When I first entered Vicki's home, the entryway and formal living room were inviting, uncluttered, calming. Those were the only rooms that reflected what Vicki wanted.

The rest of the home was cluttered with the signs of a busy, disorganized family of six. The kids ranged in age from seven to seventeen. The floors of the rooms were covered with mismatched shoes, discarded papers, worn clothes. If you opened a cabinet door or drawer, you were likely to find odds and ends, shoved in haphazardly and forgotten. Video game components and cartridges spilled out of entertainment centers. Piles of folded clothes sat on the carpeted steps to the second floor waiting for delivery. Mail, photos, phone directories, invitations, bills, takeout menus, and random notes were piled up in neat but numerous stacks on countertops. And the master bedroom was anything but the oasis Vicki and her husband needed from their chaotic lives.

Vicki's concerns were deeper than appearance, though. She felt as if her home was an incubator for stress—not a haven from it. She recognized that her family wasn't working as a team. She was convinced that if she and her family could communicate better and work together, their lives would be less stressful and she would spend less time nagging and yelling.

The day I first met Vicki had been difficult for her and her four-teen-year-old daughter,

> "Finish every day and be done with it. You have done what you could. Some blunders and absurdities no doubt crept in; forget them as soon as you can. Tomorrow is a new day."
>
> —*Ralph Waldo Emerson*

who had stayed up late and woken up early to finish a school project. Her room was littered with scraps from the project, other papers, and dirty clothes. On her way out the door, she couldn't find her soccer shorts, which she needed for that afternoon's game. Vicki joined the search, looking in every room of the house. Now her daughter was late for school, and they still couldn't find the shorts. Vicki drove to two stores on the way to school, eventually buying tape to transform plain shorts into shorts that looked like part of the uniform.

Vicki felt terrible about how the morning unraveled. She had given her other three children minimal attention and yelled at her daughter, who was in tears on her way to school—certainly not how Vicki would have preferred to handle the situation. She admitted that the episode wasn't unusual.

Vicki wasn't sure where to start—or when she'd have time—to make changes. Every week she shuttled her children to and from four different schools and various activities, worked part-time outside the home, and volunteered at multiple campuses.

Although Vicki felt as though she didn't know where to begin, she actually did. She admitted that things were out of control and asked for help—half the battle and a smart thing to do, especially when it comes to something as important as your home and the people you love.

Simple Ways to Introduce Change

Perhaps you identify with Vicki or Rachael. Maybe you feel you have so many things you want to change about your life, you don't know where to start. You can't make yourself take the first step for fear it won't be the right one. Sometimes our problems seem so interconnected that we can't see how to solve one without solving them all. We erroneously tell ourselves that until everything changes, nothing changes, so we risk nothing and resolve to live in our tangled state. Or we go to the opposite extreme and decide that no matter what, we're

"Our chief want in life is somebody who shall make us do what we can."
—Ralph Waldo Emerson

going to change everything—now. We race from problem to problem, attempting to change everything and changing nothing. Either way, we're too overwhelmed to be effective.

If you'd like to jump-start positive change in your household, consider four key steps you can begin implementing *today*. These are the same actions I, along with Family Manager Coaches Kimberly Labbe and Christi Saylors, suggested that Vicki and Rachael take first.

1. *Set up Control Central.* Every manager needs a "Control Central"—be it a desk, a countertop, or an office. In a company, it's the place from which the manager calls the shots. In a home, it's the place where the Family Manager organizes, tracks the family's schedule, notes changes, responds to messages, makes lists, and keeps all important papers in their places. By setting up your own Control Central, you can better oversee your family's comings and goings and manage the countless tasks, responsibilities, and decisions that are made every day.

   • Your Control Central could be set up on the countertop in the eating area next to your kitchen. It's a central location where you can keep your family calendar and family in-boxes. Stock the cabinet underneath with office supplies—pens, pencils, highlighters, etc.

   • Put a copy of your local phone directory here, as well as a list of the numbers your family regularly calls.

- Keep an ongoing grocery and personal-needs list here so family members will always know where to add items you're running low on.

- Have an easy-access file for takeout menus.

- Keep a trash can close by.

2. *Use a Daily Hit List.* This is different than a typical to-do list. A Daily Hit List brings sense to your day by categorizing your many jobs in the seven Family Manager departments you oversee in your home. Using a Daily Hit List will:

- declutter your mind by providing a systematic way to sort through the myriad chores and responsibilities that crowd in every morning

- clear your perspective, revealing what's trivial and what's priority

- clarify which tasks only you can do and which can be delegated or shared

- improve your memory through the exercise of writing down details

- help you remember what steps to take today so whatever's coming tomorrow will go smoothly

DAILY HIT LIST

DATE: _____

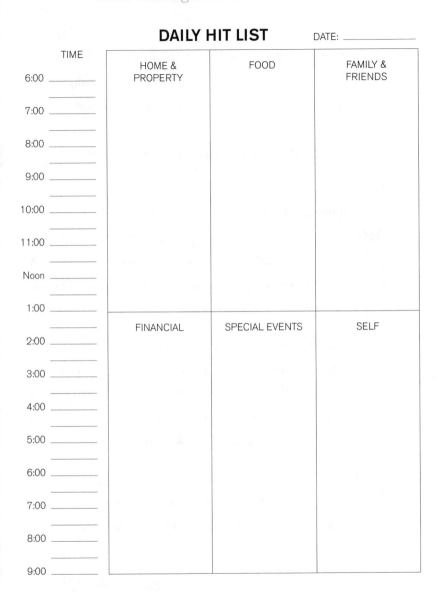

TIME			
	HOME & PROPERTY	FOOD	FAMILY & FRIENDS
6:00			
7:00			
8:00			
9:00			
10:00			
11:00			
Noon			
1:00			
	FINANCIAL	SPECIAL EVENTS	SELF
2:00			
3:00			
4:00			
5:00			
6:00			
7:00			
8:00			
9:00			

As you begin to use a Daily Hit List, accept the reality that you won't always be able to check off all of the tasks on your list at the end of the day. Move unaccomplished tasks to the next day's list, or delete the ones you deem unimportant for now.

There are three steps for making a Daily Hit List work:

Do

Think about and list *everything* that needs to be done. This includes obvious things like meals for the kids, gas for the car, and money in the bank, as well as other responsibilities such as running errands, carpooling, and scheduling appointments.

Delegate

Looking at your list, ask yourself, *What can I delegate?* Can your teenage daughter start a load of laundry before she leaves for school? Can your younger daughter fold clothes when she gets home from school? Can your teenage son go to the grocery store on his way home from practice?

Delete

Once you've delegated, take another look at the list. Are some of the tasks really expendable? What is truly unnecessary, at least for today?

3. *Call a family meeting.* Find a time when the whole family will be at home. Ask family members to share their opinions about what would make home a good place. Listen

carefully. It's important that they know you care what they think. Use a "Who's Responsible for What" list (see pages 66–67) to educate them about what needs to be done to keep your household running. Ask for volunteers to pick up some of the tasks, and if no one offers, assign jobs.

4. *Work your way through your house, organizing one area at a time.* Make "Eliminate and concentrate" your motto. *Eliminate* what you don't want, need, or use. *Concentrate* on what you use, need, and care about. For every underused item in your house, ask these clutter control questions:

- When is the last time it was used? worn? played with?

- Does it deserve space in our home? If it weren't here, what would be here instead?

- Are there memories attached to it?

- What will I do with it? Fix it, sell it, store it, toss it, or donate it?

Both Vicki and Rachael love their new Control Central. All the information they need to manage their family's schedule and the details of their lives is now in one central place. Family members know to put messages, grocery store requests, and schedule changes here. Both women also started using a Daily

Hit List to help them manage the myriad responsibilities of their days.

In Vicki's case, she conducted a family meeting at the dinner table on a night when all six of them could attend. She invited each family member to describe what would make life at home better. They told her that they would like to be able to find things such as school supplies, clothes, and shoes more easily. They wanted a quicker turnaround on laundry. They wanted less nagging. Vicki took notes of their requests, never appearing defensive or challenging their responses.

> Establish an in-and-out rule. Every time a new item comes into the house, show an old item the door. Make your family motto "Put it up, not down." Start the routine of returning everything you get out back to where it belongs. (Ten minutes a day looking for misplaced items wastes sixty hours a year.)

She had made copies of the "Who's Responsible for What" list, and after everyone had had their say, she gave a copy of the list to each family member. They were amazed at the length of the list. She was encouraged when they volunteered to help with chores.

Kimberly continued to work with Vicki, helping her clean out and organize closets in every room. Vicki says it has been a major positive life change for her and her family.

Finding the Courage to Change

Many women aren't as brave as Vicki and Rachael. They would rather play it safe, stay in their comfort zones, and tolerate the status quo instead of admitting that things need to change, asking for help, and doing what it takes to make things change.

When you take action to change something, especially something as important as your home and life, there are risks. Creating new possibilities requires you (and your family) to move outside your comfort zone, which very likely may be the cause of your discomfort in the first place. Replacing an ingrained habit with a new, healthier one can be painful at first. Making suggestions about changing the way they live can invite criticism from family members. Sadly, the potential discomfort associated with taking risks prevents many people from moving off dead center. Can you relate to these rationalizations?

- It's easier to clean the floor yourself than to patiently teach your child to do it.

- It's easier to sit and watch TV than to get up, call your neighbor, and plan a time to walk tomorrow morning.

- It's easier to pick up the phone and complain to your friend about how messy your house is than to set aside twenty minutes to work on one area.

Makeover Strategies for Good Time Management

PROBLEM

You have small children, and inevitably you lose time and run late because of an unexpected spill, a dirty diaper, or a whining toddler.

SOLUTION

Be prepared. Build buffer time into your schedule for mishaps. Stock your car with diapers and wet wipes, a roll of paper towels, a change of clothes for the kids, plastic containers filled with nonperishable snacks, and bottled water.

PROBLEM

Whenever you think about undertaking a major task, like redecorating your bathroom, you're overwhelmed.

SOLUTION

Make the steps to completing a large task tangible. List each step you'll need to accomplish your goal. As you finish each, give yourself the satisfaction of checking it off in red ink! Do the hardest part first. The rest will seem easier.

PROBLEM

Your housework is really piling up. You just keep procrastinating and feel guiltier by the day.

SOLUTION

Start using the Power of Ten principle. Spend ten minutes every day on something you've been procrastinating about. Stop and pat yourself on the back when you finish a segment of a task. If you have six drawers to clean out, congratulate yourself each time you conquer one.

GOAL: *Optimize my use of time and control stress so that I make the best use of my resources—and enjoy my life as I live it!*

PROBLEM

When you call to arrange for a haircut, your favorite stylist is always booked for weeks. You have the same problem when it's time for child's immunizations.

SOLUTION

When you get a haircut or some other service you'll need again soon, schedule your next appointment as you pay. Ditto at your pediatrician's office.

PROBLEM

Your kids always get to bed late because they can't finish their homework or find their baseball jersey at a reasonable hour.

SOLUTION

Help kids learn to estimate how long it will take them to finish their homework. Explain the importance of doing advance work, such as making sure their sports uniforms are clean before a game. Teach them to multitask while they watch TV. They can clean out their backpacks or oil their baseball gloves during their favorite shows.

PROBLEM

You're always running late in the morning because your child is never ready on time.

SOLUTION

Many times suffering the consequences is the best teacher. If your kids constantly run late before school, don't "save" them. One trip to the principal's office might be all it takes to make them prompt. Also, be sure to model the desired behavior. If they often see you procrastinating or running late, don't expect them to behave differently.

- It's easier to put off making appointments for things you know you should do—get a mammogram, a physical, or a teeth cleaning—than to sit down with your calendar and schedule them.

- It's easier to keep picking up takeout food on your way home than to sit down on Sunday night and plan menus for the week.

- It's easier to keep traveling to your sister-in-law's for the holidays and come back home exhausted than to tell her you and your family need some time alone this year.

Be Smart about Change

Realize that your family may not jump up and down with excitement at the thought of making changes around the house. As a matter of fact, they may resist your efforts. For example, if you decide to start cooking healthier so you and your family will feel better, your sixteen-year-old son who is addicted to junk food probably won't appreciate this change. If you decide to work out at the Y at 5:30 a.m. three days a week, your husband may not like hearing the alarm go off at 5 a.m., even though he's glad you care about getting into shape. It's not

"Change is not made without inconvenience, even from worse to better."
—Richard Hooker

that your son and husband don't want change; they're just concerned about how the changes will affect their world.

It is human nature to resist change, especially abrupt or forced change. It's important to put ourselves in the shoes of those affected by our changes and try to understand what they think and feel. Let's say you launch your new healthy-eating plan in a big way and immediately purge your kitchen of all products made from refined sugar or flour. You don't consider that rice cakes and whole-wheat pretzels aren't exactly what your son and his football teammates are craving when they raid your pantry after practice.

"Behold the turtle. He makes progress only when he sticks his neck out."

—James Bryant Conant

Or maybe your husband is trying to finish a big project at work and must stay up late at night to meet a deadline. When your alarm goes off at 5 a.m., maybe he has only been asleep for three hours. Whatever the scenario, it's important to be considerate of the lives and schedules of others when making changes. Keep some teen-friendly snacks around and introduce new healthy options slowly. Put your alarm clock in the bathroom and be as quiet as a mouse when you get out of bed to turn it off and get dressed. Get your exercise clothes out the night before so you don't have to rummage through your drawers looking for your sports bra and a matching pair of socks.

Whatever the change you've decided to make in your life, in order to avoid or reduce the resistance of others, ask yourself these questions:

1. Who else will be affected by the change?
2. What reasons for resistance should I anticipate?
3. What methods can I use to introduce the change that could minimize the resistance?

Most people accept change better if they are involved in the process; are asked to contribute their feelings, opinions, and suggestions; and are told the reasons for and advantages of the change.

> "Every noble work is at first impossible."
> —Thomas Carlyle

And be careful not to sabotage your own efforts to change. Don't have unrealistic expectations, and don't try to change too many things too fast. If you do, it will be easy to become discouraged and give up on making any change at all. Set realistic goals about how much you can do and how long it will take. Don't try to paint your house before your in-laws arrive this weekend or lose twenty pounds before a reunion that's coming up in a month. You'll likely end up discouraged.

A Call for Help

Not everyone can win a makeover contest, but everyone can call for help. It's easier to accomplish tasks in teams. Strength or willpower naturally increases with numbers, and our odds for success increase. A Family Manager Coach or a friend who is willing to be an accountability buddy—in other words, someone who is committed to your success—can be an encourager and cheerleader to inspire you when you're flagging. Plus, sharing your progress and your shortfalls with someone else can help you be honest with yourself and make you more likely to follow through. That's what friends—and Family Manager Coaches—are for!

Personal Reflection

Carve out some time to think about the changes you would like to make in your home. Evaluate how things are going in each Family Manager department and envision where you would like them to be. Are there some areas that are dangerously out of line, causing you and your family pain and discomfort?

"Be strong and courageous. Do not be terrified; do not be discouraged, for the LORD your God will be with you wherever you go." (Joshua 1:9)

What small step could you take today to begin changing things for the better at home? Ask God to give you the will and courage to do so.

> **About the time we think we can make ends meet, someone moves the ends.**
> Herbert Hoover

> **Beware of little expenses. A small leak will sink a great ship.**
> Benjamin Franklin

> **She watches over the affairs of her household and does not eat the bread of idleness.**
> Proverbs 31:27

CHAPTER 11

Financial Makeover

Painless Ways to Save
Hundreds of Dollars Each Month

Every Family Manager needs to be a money manager. You have to know how to stretch dollars, get the bills paid, and keep debt down. You also have to plan for the future and be prepared for out-of-the-ordinary expenses, since cars don't last forever, roofs need to be replaced, and families like to take vacations. If all this gives you goose bumps, don't be intimidated—just keep reading.

Remember this foundational truth of the Family Management system: No Family Manager is equally proficient in each of the seven departments she oversees. After the Food department, I'm least skilled in the Financial department. I have made a lot of progress, though. And I can confidently say that you don't have to be a Wall Street wizard to do a good job overseeing money matters in your home.

For years I felt threatened and unqualified when it came

to managing money. Banking information seemed to be written in a foreign language, a language I was sure every other adult in the world was conversant in. "I'm not a numbers person," I used to say. But in the early years of my career as a Family Manager, when Bill was working and taking a full load of classes in graduate school, I became the numbers person in our family by default. And that's how I made decisions too—by default. I made a lot of mistakes and got angry because all the responsibility ended up with me. I began to understand how marriages end up on the rocks as a result of money issues.

Many of our money problems were due to my tendency to procrastinate over the financial matters that I knew little about and that felt overwhelming. Sometimes my unwillingness to tackle a financial task or make a timely decision cost us a lot more money—and time—in the long run, causing even more strain on our budget and our relationship.

Eventually we decided it would be best if we split up the financial management in our home. Bill would pay the mortgage, insurance, and utilities—the monthly stuff—out of one account. I opened a special household checking account to pay for groceries, clothing, haircuts, school needs, and the like. I have one friend who uses what she calls her "envelope method." At the first of every month, she withdraws the cash she needs to pay for her family's household expenses (not bills) for a month. She puts budgeted amounts in labeled envelopes—groceries, drugstore items, entertainment, school supplies, clothing, babysitting, miscellaneous—and keeps them in a drawer. She pays cash for everything, and when the money is gone for the month, it's gone.

Frankly, I would have rather just thrown all financial responsibility into Bill's lap and never worried another second about it. But I knew I needed to buck up and learn to be a good manager of our resources. I also needed to be prepared for the worst-case scenario—if Bill dies before I do and I am left alone to deal with my family's financial affairs.

As I began to study and feel more competent and comfortable with managing money, it dawned on me that we weren't talking about the federal budget. We were talking about one family and how we made, saved, and spent our money while living on planet Earth. One family, one budget. It could, I told myself, be done.

I decided that instead of looking at finances as a complex, intimidating area of our life, I would

"An investment in knowledge always pays the best interest."
—Benjamin Franklin

look at it like a jigsaw puzzle and work on the "edges" of the problem. I tackled the pieces that I understood—getting the most for our money at the grocery store, watching for sales before purchasing items, setting up a simple filing system, and gathering and reading information about saving and investing. I found that the more I did, the less complex and overwhelming the rest of the department seemed. I became comfortable asking questions, learning a little at a time and getting the department in order a little at a time—which, by the way, is the best way to approach any department in your home (at least until a good fairy comes along with her magic wand to instantly put everything in order).

Jessica's Story

Jessica is typical of so many women whose families have been impacted by unemployment. When I met Jessica, she had recently lost her job as an administrative assistant when her company downsized. She had mixed emotions about her layoff. On one hand, she was relieved because she didn't like that her three-year-old daughter went to day care or that her thirteen-year-old stepson had to come home from school to an empty house. Now she could be there for both of them.

On the other hand, she and her husband, Doug, counted on her salary. Although not huge, her paycheck paid for any extras—entertainment, eating out, decorating the house, vacations, and such. It would be impossible for them to stay in their home and maintain their present lifestyle if she didn't find another job—or so she thought.

I explained to Jessica that the first step in solving a problem or making a good decision is to assess the facts—and to do this we needed to collect as much relevant information about her situation as possible.

First we had to determine how much money they had to

"find" for their monthly cash inflow and outflow to remain stable if she did not go back to work. To come up with this number, we took her take-home pay and subtracted costs for fuel, parking, work clothes, dry cleaning, food (lunches and snacks), and child care. We also took out a lump sum for takeout foods, eating out, and the pricier convenience foods from the grocery store she relied on to simplify some of the dinners she prepared at home. In the process of figuring out these amounts, Jessica was shocked to learn how much it was "costing" her to go to work every day!

> "I can account for every dime I spend. It's those twenties and fifties where things start getting a little foggy."
> —Martha Bolton

We made it our goal to find $800, give or take a little, by looking for places where dollars were slipping through the cracks. We didn't have to look hard to find money that was being inadvertently wasted—particularly in energy-deficient areas of their home and through poor spending decisions often made unconsciously. We discussed how these expenses could be curtailed with very little (if any) effect on their lifestyle.

Her family embraced the idea of Jessica making her full-time job managing their home and resources, and they agreed to work as a family to make up for the lost income. Her husband and stepson took on the challenge to make their home as energy efficient as possible. They put insulation in the attic, caulked windows, and fixed dripping faucets and leaking toilets. The next month they saw a noticeable decrease in their utility bills.

Jessica focused on planning meals and becoming a shrewd grocery shopper. She found that she enjoyed the challenge . . . and her family enjoyed many more home-cooked meals. Her new schedule allowed her to do some research and compare the costs for long-distance and cell phone service, cable service, credit card amenities and interest rates, homeowners and automobile insurance, and bank fees. Until then, she had wondered if they were paying premium prices for these things, and she had wanted to look into getting better deals. She just couldn't find the time to do so. Her instincts proved correct, and her research reaped lower rates in all areas.

She also had more time to get to know her neighbors. She put her administrative gifts to work and organized a neighborhood garage sale and a babysitting co-op.

Even if you don't have the time that Jessica now has to closely monitor expenses, you can make some relatively simple changes that will save you money. In fact, you don't have to spend hours to get your financial "house" in order. Time is treasure, as the old adage goes, and by learning to use instead of spend small bits of both time and treasure, you can prevail over paperwork, stretch dollars to buy what you need now, learn to save what you need for the future—and end up with change!

Power of Ten Cash Savers

- Take ten minutes to open a savings account at a bank branch inside your grocery store. When you buy groceries, instead of having coupon amounts deducted from your bill, ask for the refund in cash. Then walk directly to the in-store bank and deposit the money. (If your store doesn't have a bank, you could take ten minutes to stop by your bank on the way home from the store.) That dream vacation will become a reality before you know it!

- Limit trips to the ATM. Take ten minutes to estimate all the cash you will need for the next week or two. Store cash in an envelope in a secure place. Keep a pen handy to jot down how much and when you or family members take out cash so you can track spending.

- Before you shop for a car, household appliances, and just about anything else, take ten minutes to do comparison shopping online. You can save big bucks.

Makeover Strategies for Setting and Reaching Financial Objectives

PROBLEM

Your work hours have just been unexpectedly cut, and you don't know how you'll be able to cover the mortgage each month.

SOLUTION

Before panicking, realize that by breaking down larger financial challenges into smaller pieces, they become less daunting. For instance, to reduce spending by $500 a month, you'll need to cut spending by $16.66 a day. Brainstorm ways you might do so. Could you drop (or scale back on) your Internet or cable service? Could you carpool? eat out less often?

PROBLEM

The totals due on your credit cards each month seem to be spiraling out of control.

SOLUTION

Think twice before putting anything on a credit card, since it is one of the costliest ways to obtain credit. Also, use one low-interest credit card that gives you air miles or points for other purchases rather than multiple high-interest cards. Finally, remember that banks and credit card companies make mistakes. Check your bills carefully.

PROBLEM

You often find yourself regretting a purchase that you felt you had to have while in the store.

SOLUTION

A good way to get perspective before making a purchase is to consider how many hours you'd need to work to pay for something you want to buy. For example, if you earn $15 an hour and an item costs $120, ask yourself if what you want is worth eight hours of work.

GOAL: *Get your family's spending and saving habits under control.*

PROBLEM
You'd love to go to an amusement park or on a short getaway with your family, but you just don't see how you could ever fit it into your budget.

SOLUTION
Begin collecting the change from your purse or pockets at the end of each day. On average, Americans carry $1.28 in change, so if you save $1.28 a day for 365 days, you'll have $467.20! Get your family in on the fun, and save for something special.

PROBLEM
You're never sure how much money is really going in and out each month.

SOLUTION
To track your finances more accurately, buy a home-budget software system for your computer. Take some time each month to update your records and observe spending patterns.

PROBLEM
You feel as if your family's finances are totally out of control. You have creditors calling, and you're not sure how you can possibly meet this month's rent and credit card payments.

SOLUTION
Realize that you won't make the problems go away by ignoring them. Often it is best to call your creditors and explain the problem. You may be able to work out a payment plan, since companies much prefer a partial payment to no payment at all. If you need additional counsel, don't be afraid to seek it.

Becoming a Good Money Manager

A key reason Jessica and Doug were able to adapt to becoming a one-income family was because they agreed to work together to stretch Doug's income. This would allow Jessica to be home with their kids, which they felt was more important than her paycheck at this time in life. This decision influenced all of their other financial decisions.

Likewise, if you want to get the Financial department of your family under control, you must decide what's most important to you. Some people value sending their children to private schools; others value a nice home or prize memorable family vacations. And for many families, just having enough money to pay the bills and make ends meet until the next paycheck has great value. None of these things are wrong in and of themselves; you just have to decide how each fits into your priorities and lifestyle.

Every day we're bombarded with messages designed to persuade us to believe propositions that aren't true at all. Television commercials and glossy magazine ads show us how our homes are "supposed" to look. They suggest we would feel better about ourselves and about life if only we had this or that. Redo and be happy. Bigger is better. Newest and latest is best. Trade in, trade up. Excess becomes ideal. Invention becomes the mother of necessity—or so we think.

Unless we've made some decisions about what we deem important, it's easy to lose perspective, make impulsive

Painless Ways to Save Money

You can cut energy costs with these easy steps:

- Keep windows and doors near the thermostat closed. Cool or warm air will make your heater or air conditioner work harder.
- Replace air conditioner and heater filters every month when they are in use.
- Seal your windows with caulk and weather stripping.
- Set your refrigerator thermostat at 40 degrees. (Most are set at 32 degrees.)
- It costs more for your freezer to be half full than to be completely filled. Fill it with sacks of ice or other items that take up space.
- Lower the temperature of your water heater to 120 degrees.
- Check for toilet leaks. Put a few drops of food coloring in your toilet tank. If is shows up in the bowl, there's a leak. An average leak can waste ten gallons of water per hour.
- Save ten gallons of water each day by cutting two minutes off your shower time.

Consider these ways to scale back on service expenses without any noticeable effect:

- Ask your insurance agent about ways to decrease your premiums, such as installing smoke alarms or having a student driver with a good report card.
- Schedule appointments for haircuts and highlights at a beauty school instead of a high-end salon.
- Look into joining your local YMCA or community center instead of a pricey health club. These places often provide the same services for a lot less.
- Avoid clothing that requires dry cleaning. It's like being forced to pay five to ten dollars every time you wear the outfit.

decisions, and spend money that we shouldn't spend. If money is tight and we haven't decided what we value in life, we can easily feel insecure, discontented, and unable to enjoy the blessings we have.

Here's one way this played out in my family. Early in our marriage, Bill and I decided that a good investment would be to spend money on making memories with our children. When we had the choice of taking a family trip or putting more money into savings or buying a new piece of furniture, we decided we'd go for the trip and deposit memories in our kids' mental and emotional savings account. Thirty-six years later, our savings account at the bank is nothing to write home about, but we have a huge account of great family memories. Plus, we have a wonderful relationship with each of our boys. To us, this is worth millions.

> "Command those who are rich in this present world not to be arrogant nor to put their hope in wealth, which is so uncertain, but to put their hope in God, who richly provides us with everything for our enjoyment."
> *(1 Timothy 6:17)*

Restraint is something most of us don't enjoy. But if we ever want to make progress financially, we must learn to live within our means. Establishing priorities helps us do this. I've found that it helps to look at purchases as trade-offs. Is a new house really worth the extra financial pressure the larger payments will put on our family? Is a new

More Painless Ways to Save Money

Get your family and friends involved so you can have fun while saving money:

- Have a garage sale. Begin by setting a target date. Then give yourself plenty of time and intermittent goals. For instance, if you want to have your sale on September 15, you might set aside August 30 to clean out the attic, September 2 and 3 to work through your closets, and September 7 and 8 to clean out drawers and cupboards.

- Ask a neighbor to split the cost of renting a carpet-cleaning machine for a day. Help each other move furniture around and get the job done for a lot less than hiring a professional.

- Start a toy-swapping club with other mothers. Trade toys your kids don't mind living without for a couple of weeks. The kids will love having different toys often, and you'll save money by not buying new ones.

- Invite other families to join a fruit- and vegetable-buying co-op; items can be purchased cheaper in large quantities. Each family takes a specific month to take care of shopping at a farmers' market, dividing and distributing items, and collecting money.

- Start an errand co-op with neighbors or coworkers. One person goes to the post office, another to the toy store, a third to the beauty-supply store.

- Rather than spending money going away on a romantic retreat with your spouse, trade babysitting weekends with a friend and have your weekend at home.

- Enjoy low-cost family fun. Get up early, watch the sun rise, and cook breakfast out at a park. Go on a bike-hike as a family, ride to a favorite eating spot, and then ride back. Call your local parks and recreation department and ask about inexpensive programs and activities that your family might enjoy.

car really worth not being as free to go out to eat or buy a new outfit? It's easier to make wise choices when they're based on the lifestyle we've decided on beforehand, not on impulses to have the newest, latest, or best.

In addition to considering your family priorities, ask yourself these questions before making a large purchase:

1. Do we really need it?
2. Can we make do with what we have?
3. How often will we use it?
4. How much care does it require?
5. Is it durable?
6. Does its design and quality meet our standards?
7. Is there information available to help us make our decision?
8. Is the price right? Could we find it at a secondhand store?
9. How much difference will its addition to our home and family life really make?

Think about your last sizable purchase—a new car, a new sofa, or a piece of jewelry. Did you buy it expecting it to bring you satisfaction? I've certainly done that. Did you notice how long that rush of joy over a new purchase lasted? Usually it's not long before I want something else. If you can relate, recognize this temptation and refuse to be sucked into the excitement of always getting something new. Remember that the happiness will not last as long as the payments.

File Those Paper Piles

In addition to setting priorities, it's also important that you develop a good filing and bill-paying system. If you currently "file" receipts, bills, and other important documents in piles around your house, realize that the time you invest to set

> "Few rich men own their own property. The property owns them."
>
> —*Robert G. Ingersoll*

up and maintain a good system of family files and records will pay off over and over again. You'll save time when you need to find an important document or piece of information. Never again will you have to spend two hours hunting for a medical record or a child's birth certificate.

Another important benefit of getting organized is that you will learn a lot about your family's finances. For example, while organizing your legal documents, you may discover that you didn't update your will after adding a child to the family. You may see that you could reduce your insurance costs by increasing your deductible.

A simple, organized filing system eases the stress of family emergencies such as a layoff, a severe illness, or an unexpected death. It makes tax time easier too.

Use this seven-step excavation plan to conquer the paper piles in your home.

1. Put all the papers you need to deal with or file in one place.

Get a wastebasket or recycle box, file folders, labels, pens, and a stapler.

2. Start with the first paper. Decide if it's valuable and necessary. If not, toss or recycle it. If it's worth keeping, move to step 3.

3. Choose a file heading for it, label the folder, and file the paper. You might use some of these headings: Medical Records, Personal Letters, Autos, and Decorating Ideas.

4. If there are two or more papers associated with the topic you're dealing with, staple the papers together. Don't use paper clips. They get caught on each other and fall off easily.

5. Pick up the next piece of paper and follow the same procedure, except to file it in the appropriate file if you've already created it. Consolidate as much as you can.

6. When you've gone through all your papers, sort the files according to the Family Manager departments (see below), then alphabetize the files within the departments. Place the files in a file drawer or carton.

Home & Property. Decorating ideas; trash collection and recycling information; auto information; dream house pictures and plans; gardening information; household inventory; appraisals; receipts for all home improvements, additions, and repairs.

Food. Nutritional information, takeout menus, party menus, caterers, centerpiece inspirations, recipes.

Family & Friends. Assign each family member a file folder color, and store the following in each person's files: birth certificates, immunization records, school history/report cards, résumés, hobby and sports information, prescriptions for eyeglasses and contacts, pet records. If you have children living at home, the National Center for Missing & Exploited Children recommends keeping a home identification file on each child to assist law enforcement officials in the event of a child abduction. The file should include a complete set of fingerprints as well as dental information.

Finances. Banking (checking and savings) records, spare checks, loan papers, insurance, receipts for purchases, mortgage or rental papers, tax information, investments, organizations to which you pay annual dues, retirement information, health insurance information.

Special Events. Travel, vacation research, maps and tourist information, garage sale records (what worked and what didn't work the last time you held one), birthday party and holiday ideas, holiday greeting card list, family reunion research, rental company brochures.

Time & Scheduling. Tips/articles on time management, last year's calendar, public transportation schedules.

Self-Management. Personal interests and hobbies; personal medical records; community or church volunteer papers; weight loss, beauty, and wardrobe information.

7. Purge regularly. Each time you refer to a file, thumb through it and discard any papers that no longer are necessary.

Financial management is really all about keeping on top of the details and using your priorities to guide your decisions. Come to think of it, that's not a bad way to manage any area of your household!

Personal Reflection

"Where your treasure is, there your heart will be also."
(Matthew 6:21)

The Bible has a great deal to say about money. There are five hundred verses on prayer and fewer than five hundred on faith, yet more than two thousand verses on money and possessions. Nearly half of Jesus' parables deal with how to handle money and possessions.

Whether we're aware of it or not, we live out what we believe to be true about money, all day, every day. It's important that we understand what our financial priorities are, because they will influence how we spend our money, how we spend our time, the values we pass onto our children, our future, and a host of other important issues.

Everyone is influenced to some extent by the way his or her parents handled finances and what they valued. So when two people unite in marriage, they bring with them a philosophy of money and a lot of standards they think are perfectly normal. Consider:

- What are your views regarding money?
- What are your husband's?
- Have your two views brought conflict? How?

Take some time to sit down by yourself (if you're a single parent) or with your husband and consider what the following money-related concepts mean to you. This will help you clarify your priorities.

1. List five things that you value most about your life today.

2. List five things you want that money can buy.

3. List five things you want that money can't buy.

4. How much is enough? I'll feel okay about money when we have $_____ in the bank. I'll be content when we have $_____ .

5. List the causes you'd like to give money to. How much would you like to give?

> **Too many people, too many demands, too much to do . . . it just isn't living at all.**
> Anne Morrow Lindbergh

> **Love your neighbor as yourself.**
> Matthew 19:19

> **When we love other people, we are eager and willing to spend time and energy taking care of them, meeting their needs and helping them flourish. Why should we think that to love ourselves means anything less?**
> Anonymous

CHAPTER 12

Self-Development Makeover

Finding Time to Pursue Your Dreams

No two women are alike. We have different decorating styles, fashion preferences, political persuasions, views about child rearing, and ways to make dressing at Thanksgiving. But there are at least two important things we share in common: We all have the same amount of hours in a day (just twenty-four), and no matter how busy our schedules or what kinds of responsibilities we juggle, we need to take care of ourselves. Most days that's easier said than done, since moms are known the world over for putting themselves last.

Because you're reading this book, I'm going to assume you're familiar with that feeling of regret when, at the end of the day, you realize you never got around to that walk you so desperately wanted to take. You're sad and perhaps even a little angry that you never found time to write in your prayer journal. Your mind wasn't stretched—except when you had to figure out how much of a new brand of detergent to use. You didn't get to laugh with a friend. In fact, you didn't do anything that refreshes you. And it was a fairly good day—meaning there weren't any huge catastrophes.

Then there are the days when children become ill, babysitters cancel, toilets overflow, interminable meetings eat up our time, and relatives have emergencies and need us—now. We set our jaw, switch into crisis mode, and move through the day doing whatever it takes to manage each catastrophe as it comes. The idea of stopping to recharge our own batteries doesn't cross our minds, and if it does, we quickly say to ourselves, *I'm so busy caring for everyone else, there's no way I have time to care for myself.* Putting our own needs last seems like the noble thing to do, but the truth is that when we don't take care of ourselves, we're not doing anyone a favor. When we're feeling increasingly stressed, depressed, and restless, our families can't help but know it. And if we burn out, everyone suffers.

> The way we treat ourselves will inevitably affect the way we treat others.

How do we know if we're headed for burnout? Attitude is a good litmus test. If we go to bed feeling resentful more often than fulfilled, *Houston, we have a problem.* . . .

Wake-Up Calls

It took a serious wake-up call—you know, the kind that falls into the category of radical, life-altering experiences—for me to snap to it. When our older boys were nine and five, my life was reeling out of control. The boys were involved in sports and other activities most afternoons after school. I busily ran from meetings to appointments to ball games to events. I was becoming more proficient in many areas of Family Management, but I had not yet added the Self-Management department to my system. I became overwhelmed and exhausted, and ultimately I landed in the hospital.

After undergoing numerous medical tests, I was diagnosed with chronic fatigue syndrome. I was completely drained of energy and unable to think clearly or function without pain. During the six hours a day I managed to hold my eyes open, I did a lot of thinking. I thought about how I had gotten myself into this miserable state. Was it because my calendar was booked to eternity? Because I had said yes to everyone who asked me to do anything? Because I crammed way too many things into each day—especially things I didn't enjoy but had committed to do? Because another day was over, I was exhausted, and I hadn't had even five minutes of fun? All of the above were true.

Although it was more than twenty years ago, I can still remember the day before my crash. In addition to the responsibilities of running my own home, I had attended two community service meetings, cooked and delivered dinner to two new mothers, helped a friend highlight her hair, and assisted another friend with picking out and packing clothes for a trip.

Time to Reflect

As I lay in bed, I thought about how I would spend the hours of the day if the gift of time was given back to me. I would get serious about living more in line with my priorities instead of other people's priorities for me, and I would get serious about managing myself—caring for my body, nourishing my spirit, sharpening my mind, and doing some things that recharged my batteries on a daily basis. Thankfully, in a couple of months my health returned and I began living each day as a gift. A verse in Luke became a life-shaping paradigm for me.

"Jesus grew in wisdom and stature, and in favor with God and men." (Luke 2:52)

I had used this verse as a guide in parenting our boys, setting goals for how I could help each of them grow and develop like Jesus did: mentally—learning new things and becoming wise in the art of living; physically—nourishing and caring for his body; spiritually—growing in faith and commitment to God; and socially/emotionally—learning to be a good friend to others and himself. It dawned on me that I should set goals for myself in these areas as well. I needed an uncomplicated way to build wise, healthy routines into my life. Plus, I needed to model the lifestyle and values I wanted our boys to embrace.

I set goals and established habits for myself each year in these areas so I could take daily steps to grow toward a healthier, better self. In a preemptive move for handling days when inevitable crises would arise and I would have to toss my agenda to the wind, I picked one simple thing I would do in each area to care for myself. I jealously guarded my schedule, and these stopgap measures became my "No matter whats." No matter what else happened, even on the worst of days, I would at the very least start the day with prayer, do something to better my body, learn something new, and in some way be a good friend to others and myself.

My daily disciplines included exercising, taking vitamins, eating healthy, studying the Bible, prayer journaling, taking courses,

Jesus said, "Love your neighbor as yourself." So it stands to reason that before I can love my neighbor very effectively, I have to love myself—not in a narcissistic, the-world-revolves-around-me sense, but by being my own friend, looking after myself, wishing myself well, and forgiving myself when necessary.

stepping out on dreams, and making time to have fun. One of the dreams I allowed myself to step out on was to try to write a book. As I write my nineteenth book, I'm very grateful for my wake-up call! Book writing grew into speaking, media interviews, and many more opportunities. Then a year ago I stepped out on a long-held dream to build a national community of women who are trained and certified through the online Family

Manager University to become Family Manager Coaches and perform Family Manager Makeovers. I have no doubt that God led me and other dear friends and partners to create this company. But I also have no doubt that God didn't want me to run myself into the ground doing it.

It is not without embarrassment that I tell you I'm living through my second wake-up call as I write this book. On the one hand, it was a great shock to learn in early 2007 that I have very early stage breast cancer. But on the other hand, I knew that something had to get my attention. I had been working way too hard for the past year. My regular exercise routine had gotten crowded out of my schedule. Sleeping more than five hours a night had become a distant memory.

I count it a gift from God that the minute area of carcinoma was caught so early in a routine mammogram, and there's a 100 percent cure rate. Since I received this second wake-up call, I've thought a lot about what a friend who is a counselor once told me. He said, "Don't miss the lesson" when going through difficult passages in life, because if you do, you'll likely have to retake the class. Well, this is a class I'd rather not retake, so I jumped back into my daily disciplines of taking care of my body—ASAP.

> "None of us can be a source of strength unless we nurture our own strength."
> —M. Scott Peck

I am grateful for this second wake-up call. I needed to be

jolted back to the reality that I must practice what I know to be true and teach it to other women: Valuing and caring for ourselves pays off in many ways, including being a better wife, mother, and friend—and enjoying life a whole lot more. When I met Mary Kay, she was learning this truth too.

Mary Kay's Story

"I can't believe I'm letting you see this mess," said Mary Kay as she opened the door to greet me. She was having second thoughts about allowing the world to peer into her home for an *Oprah* show. Her desperation overcame her desire to throw the production crew and me out of the house.

Understandably, she was apprehensive and embarrassed. You see, Mary Kay is one of those women who is naturally organized and loves to clean. When she and her husband first met, she was managing a bustling telecommunications office. After they married, she took pride in keeping their home spotless and organized.

When I met her ten years later at age forty-one, she was the mother of four boys ranging in age from five months to eight years old—a handful for any mom. She was trying her hardest to keep up with laundry and cleaning. As we walked through her house, I detected a faint odor in the bathrooms. She noticed me notice and quickly explained she hadn't gotten around to sanitizing the bathrooms yet that day. It turned out that her boys had poor aim, and their carelessness smelled!

I assured her that I knew the odor well, having raised three boys myself.

Mary Kay told me that for the past decade her entire life had been devoted to nurturing and caring for her beloved family and their home. Although rewarding, this business of nurturing others had zapped her identity. She was seriously worried about the effect on her once cheery personality. She didn't like who she was becoming and doubted her family did either.

"I never dreamed things could get this bad. If you can help me, you can help anyone," she said with a tinge of dare in her tone. She was desperate to carve out some time for herself. She needed to recharge her batteries, to nurture herself. "Just ten minutes of solitude sounds like a vacation to me right now," she said with all seriousness.

It was clear that Mary Kay meant business. She was ready to do whatever it took to get her personal life back on track. Fortunately, her wonderful sense of humor—the home-court advantage for any desperate housewife—remained intact.

"Restlessness and discontent are the first necessities of progress."
—Thomas Edison

As I watched Mary Kay work, it became clear why she had so little time for herself. As soon as her boys were up, she made their beds and picked up clutter. We figured out that she spent eight to ten minutes in each of the three bedrooms—twenty-

four to thirty minutes a day. We quickly talked about transfer-
ring this responsibility to the boys.

She also washed, dried, and folded two loads of laundry every day. She spent ten minutes gathering, sorting, and loading
the washer, and four minutes moving clothes from the washer
to the dryer and hanging the non-dryer items. We calculated
fourteen minutes for folding and putting away each load, total-
ing forty-two minutes a day for laundry—not counting ironing.
The boys could help by bringing their dirty clothes to the laundry room. They could also fold towels, socks, and underwear
while watching TV. Time reaped for Mary Kay: ten to fifteen
minutes a day.

Each day Mary Kay spent twenty minutes or more cleaning
and sanitizing their three bathrooms. I suggested she try "target practice," keeping a container of O-shaped cereal on the
back of the toilet and teaching the boys to drop one in the toi-
let-bowl water and try to hit it. She could also keep premoist-
ened antibacterial wipes in the bathroom and have them wipe
off the rim and seat, then wash their hands when finished.

Mary Kay tends by nature to be an overcleaner. She vacuumed every day, and when she saw a spare minute, she looked
for something to clean—and with four boys, there's always
something. I suggested she lower her standards. Having
four boys means a home will never be perfectly clean—and
that's okay.

Next she and I worked on a plan to free up an hour every

Makeover Strategies for Finding Time for You

PROBLEM

You've become your children's personal maid.

SOLUTION

Establish rules about how many toys can be out at one time. Have your children spend a few minutes picking up their rooms before bedtime. Purchase comforters instead of bedspreads to simplify bed making, and don't use a top sheet. Put a small laundry basket in each child's closet. Teach kids to bring dirty clothes to the laundry area twice weekly.

PROBLEM

You spend time chatting, usually about unimportant things, with just about anyone who calls during the day.

SOLUTION

Break the "I have to answer the phone" habit. Use voice mail or turn on the answering machine every morning to screen calls. Use a portable phone and accomplish something around the house—load dishes into the dishwasher, fold clothes, sort mail—while chatting with friends at designated times.

PROBLEM

You've put on a few pounds since the birth of your last child, so searching for something to wear every morning is taking too much time.

SOLUTION

Purchase a few new "workout friendly" items to put on in the morning. Adopt an "attitude of exercise" while doing housework—bending, stretching, and making every move count. Don't feel guilty about spending time each day on the treadmill, even if toys and stray socks are cluttering the floor.

GOAL: *Find an hour every day for self-care and development.*

PROBLEM

You've finally found a way to make exercise a regular part of your life again. Every day after you finish your household chores, you reward yourself by putting your toddler in a jogging stroller and heading for the park. Then your neighbor calls to say she's starting a morning aerobics class at the local YMCA and hopes you'll support her by signing up.

SOLUTION

If you look forward to your morning trips to the park and are mortified by the idea of stretching and bending in front of other women, don't feel obligated to sign up for that class. You need to be sure to make time for activities that you enjoy. That's especially true of exercise, which is vital to your overall health.

PROBLEM

You're generally so wiped out that when you finally do have a few minutes of free time, you just plop in front of the TV with a bowl of ice cream.

SOLUTION

Like anything else in your life, self-care may take some advance thought. Start by jotting down ten things you have the most fun doing, along with the last time you did them. Be sure to schedule some time this week to do one of them—preferably the one you did longest ago.

PROBLEM

You're bored with your life.

SOLUTION

Whether you sign up for a class at a local college or fitness center or simply try to read one interesting book a month, you'll find that life is much richer when you're stretching your mind or body. (Spending just five minutes a day to grow intellectually amounts to thirty hours a year of "class time.")

day that Mary Kay could use for self-care and development. We identified some habits that were robbing her of time throughout the day. We talked about the importance of lowering her standards (striving for a perfectly clean house with four boys is enough to make anyone lose emotional equilibrium!), and we also discussed how to encourage her boys to help with some of the housework. The new way of doing things proved to be emotionally freeing for Mary Kay. But the changes went deeper than that. Through the makeover project, she began to realize that it was okay to feel as if something was missing from her life—something she had felt guilty about up to this point.

After making some of my suggested changes, Mary Kay found an hour or more each day to concentrate on some activities she felt might be personally renewing and rewarding.

"We all struggle with that—what's going to make us happy, make us fulfilled," she said. "I had some things on my mind I wanted to at least try."

In addition to spending some time exercising and stopping to rest and reflect for a few minutes during the day, her "found time" allowed her to volunteer at her boys' school. She and a friend spent a year researching and creating a proposal for an after-school book club. She enjoyed this immensely. The school board embraced the program, and the club launched with about thirty elementary school students.

Her creativity continued to blossom, and she created a game for the club to engage the kids and encourage discussion. The kids liked the game immediately, and it turned out to be so popular that another volunteer asked her to adapt the game for use with Alzheimer's patients. The wheels in Mary Kay's head started turning faster. She wondered what it would take to develop a multipurpose game and get it into stores. She researched the game market, developed a number of applications, and tested her game, Kubit2me, with focus groups.

"My makeover went much deeper than finding time to work out. It was more a self-realization and finding out what I was called to do. The makeover proved to me that anything is possible if you can carve out some time to care for yourself and pursue your dreams," Mary Kay said.

Finding Time for You

Now let's work on finding time for you to care for yourself and grow toward your own personal best. In addition to building some time-saving routines into your day like Mary Kay did, think about the following five strategies in light of your own circumstances. Learning how you tick will help you get control of the clock.

1. Let first things be first.

I've said it before and I'll say it again. Pure and simple, managing time is a matter of priorities. You have to decide what really matters to you—the quality of life you desire for your family and yourself, what kind of relationship you want with your husband, the values and memories you want your children to take with them when they leave home, the gifts and dreams you want to pursue. Then you have to say no to requests that do not reflect your priorities. Period. When you say yes to something, you're saying no to something else.

2. Keep your goals and priorities front and center.

Purposely think about your goals and priorities daily until they become woven into the fabric of your being. Post them in places where you can see them regularly, such as on your bathroom mirror, on your closet wall, on your desk, or in the front of your calendar notebook—or make them your computer wallpaper or screen saver. This will remind you to use your time wisely each day and make good decisions about short- and long-term projects.

Sometimes it helps to think of time as a commodity, like money. For example, when you break down each month's salary and decide how much money you will use for vital things such as groceries and utilities, you may end up hungry and reading in the dark if you decide on a whim to buy pricey new dining room furniture. In much the same way, if you join a Pilates class that meets on Mondays and Thursdays at noon and you sign up for choir on Wednesday nights because you love to sing and enjoy the people in the choir, don't let a manipulative neighbor guilt you into chairing a big community fund-raising event that requires meeting on Wednesday nights and Thursdays at noon for the next three months unless you feel specifically called to do this. Just make sure you say no to something else so you can yes to yourself elsewhere.

3. Learn to reset your start button.

When your schedule gets overloaded, take a short break and do something that refreshes you. (This presupposes that you know the types of activities that energize you as well as the types that drain you.) The point is, don't assume you have to go through your days feeling drained and unmotivated. In fact, while going back to bed might seem mighty appealing some days, unless you're actually sick, you'd probably be better off deciding whether something else is triggering your lethargy:

Thirst. You lose the equivalent of ten cups of water from everyday living. And you replace only about four through eating. Hidden dehydration robs you of energy and makes you feel lethargic.

Darkness. When it's dark, your body says, "Sleep." When it's light, your body says, "Get up and move!" When you get up in the morning, throw open the curtains or turn on the lights immediately. Get as much light as you can, and you'll feel more energetic!

High-fat diet. Have you ever finished a meal and wanted to go and lie down? That's probably because you fed your body high-fat foods, which tend to make us lethargic.

Poor sleep habits. If you don't sleep consistently at the same time for at least eight hours, you are probably throwing your body out of whack. It doesn't know when it's supposed to be awake and when it's supposed to be asleep. Sleep isn't an indulgence; it's a necessity!

TV watching. When you feed your mind with television, you are encouraging your body to be passive. Even "smart" shows, such as History Channel programs or the evening news, can zap energy because they turn your body to sedentary mode. So watch television in moderation, and make sure you're being active the rest of the time.

Inactivity. If you don't use it, you lose it. Even little things such as climbing stairs or carrying heavy groceries can zap your energy if you don't regularly use your body in other ways. So walk, run, bike, play tag with your kids, or do anything else to get your body moving.

It's also important to know what replenishes you. Here are some that work for me, but you know yourself best. Think about what gives you an energy boost.

1. Spend some time outdoors. Breathe some fresh air and feel the sunshine.
2. Make a list of the little blessings in your life from this past week. If none come to mind, ask yourself some questions: Has your car been running smoothly? Do you have hot

water for a shower? Don't forget the things we tend to take for granted—two eyes, two hands, two feet, and a brain.

3. Start working on a project or putter at a hobby you enjoy.

4. Find a special place that refreshes and inspires you, whether it's a park bench, a mountain trail, the beach, or the woods. Use it as a regular retreat in which to read or reflect.

5. Schedule a quiet time every day, and say no to interruptions. If you retreat to the bathroom to soak in the tub, put a "Do Not Disturb" sign on the door. Young children who don't take naps can be taught that even if they don't go to sleep, they must have quiet time in their own rooms looking at books, listening quietly to CDs or tapes, or playing with quiet toys.

6. Go on a short vacation by yourself, even if it's just for a day or two. Even if you've taken a family vacation recently, you need a vacation from your job as Family Manager.

7. Plan for free time. Block it out on your calendar just as you would an important appointment.

8. Start an informal support group. Seek out like women and agree to be there for each other when life gets tough.

9. Exercise. When we exercise, our metabolism and energy level increase.

4. Know your "no matter whats."

"No matter whats" are the things that you are going to do today one way or the other, no matter what the day brings. These are your self-care routines that act as your personal life support system. For example, you might decide that no matter how busy you get, you're going to always take time to pray, exercise, or spend a few minutes caring for your skin.

5. Identify habits that waste minutes in your day.

If you're spending dangerously little time on taking care of yourself and you're feeling close to meltdown, you need to be painfully honest about identifying the time robbers in your life. You know, things like watching useless TV, surfing the Internet, chatting on the phone, being a personal maid to family members, searching for misplaced items, and so on. You may discover that you're committing a lot of time to nonpriority activities or doing things for other people that they can do for themselves. If you sense you're wasting a lot of time each day, review chapter 10.

> The essence of foolishness is that either we don't recognize the truth or we choose to ignore it. Honestly evaluate how you might be wasting time.

6. Practice "executive neglect."

This is a strategy executives use when they purposefully neglect certain issues and tasks so they can focus on other more important ones. This allows them to spend their time and energy focusing on their vision and mission. Family Managers can benefit from this concept too. There simply are not enough hours in the day and enough of you to satisfy every person and cause vying for your time and energy.

Executive neglect means that you don't volunteer for a project just because there's a need or because a colleague is putting pressure on you or because you signed up to help for the past three years and people expect you to do so again. It means that you carefully assess each opportunity and target your efforts toward projects that reap the most benefit for the time and energy you spend.

A simple cost-benefit analysis will help you evaluate volunteer opportunities. Before you say yes, ask yourself three questions:

1. Am I passionate about the cause? If you're disappointed that your college alumni association voted to enhance campus landscaping rather than give another scholarship, don't volunteer to help raise funds.

2. What will it cost me time-wise? In addition to the actual time you spend volunteering, figure in travel time and any extra time you'll need to change clothes, pick up a babysitter, and the like.

3. What are the potential benefits? For example, let's say you want to get more involved in your church and you've been asked to serve on the missions committee, which meets twice a month on Monday nights. This would mean spending more time away from your family. You also learn that the youth pastor is looking for adult volunteers to

accompany students to the homeless shelter where they serve dinner on Wednesday nights. When weighing the benefits of the two options, you realize that since your son is involved in the youth group, you'd get to spend time with him and share the satisfaction of helping others together— an additional benefit.

I hope you'll come back to this chapter when you're tempted to put your own needs on the back burner. Keep in mind that your children do not need a cranky, resentful, overworked, "unfun" mom. They need somebody who can be present for them.

Personal Reflection ✳

Is there a desire in your heart, a dream you want to pursue? The most important thing you can do is to turn your dream and your waiting over to God on a day-by-day basis. Be faithful to do what you've been given to do today, and in faith spend some time each day praying about your dream and preparing yourself to step out on the dream when the time is right.

> "'I know the plans I have for you,' declares the LORD, 'plans to prosper you and not to harm you, plans to give you hope and a future.'" (Jeremiah 29:11)

Take time to ask God to show you what you can do to move a little toward your dream and become the woman He created you to be.

> **The healthy, the strong individual, is the one who asks for help when he needs it. Whether he has an abscess on his knee or in his soul.**
Rona Barrett

....

> **Asking for help does not mean that we are weak or incompetent. It usually indicates an advanced level of honesty and intelligence.**
Anne Wilson Schaef

....

> **Two are better than one, because they have a good return for their work. . . . If two lie down together, they will keep warm. But how can one keep warm alone? Though one may be overpowered, two can defend themselves. A cord of three strands is not quickly broken.**
Ecclesiastes 4:9, 11–12

CHAPTER 13

How Desperate Are You?

Power That Produces Change

The common denominator of the women whose stories you've read is that they were desperate for change and ready to make it happen. Not all women are like this. I meet many women who have adopted a victim mentality. They feel stuck, discontented. They complain about their husband, children, house, job, bank account, and lack of happiness. I find myself in this frame of mind at times, and I don't like my own company when I'm there.

All of us get stuck every once in a while. Our vision becomes blurred. Our courage starts to wane. Our problems—some of which are real, some of which are exaggerated, and some of which are imagined—seem bigger than life. We can't see how our circumstances will ever change. We don't see that we have choices and feel as though things are reeling out of control. We lose the ability to dream of a better life.

Every positive change in life—from enhancing the

atmosphere of our homes to learning to work as a family team to reducing monthly expenses and saving for a family cruise—

Some things are outside of our control, such as our age, our physical capabilities, and other people's choices. But countless things in our lives are within our control, such as our attitudes, our priorities, and at least some of the hours of each day.

starts with a dream, a vision for something better. But not all women feel the freedom to dream. Some are so burdened by responsibilities or heartache that they can hardly see beyond today, much less dream about tomorrow. All they see is the carpet that needs replacing, the stack of unpaid bills, the hands on the clock reminding them that their teenager has missed curfew again. Other women have come to believe that dreaming of a better life is for other people who belong to a more privileged class. This was the case with my friend Erin.

Erin's Story

Erin never allowed herself to dream that she could have a better life until she was twenty-seven years old. At that time she was broke, eight months pregnant, living in cramped military quarters, and ready to divorce her pilot husband, whom she rarely saw. Life was hard, and it had been ever since her father had died, leaving her mother and the six children almost penniless. From the age of ten, Erin did odd jobs until she was old enough to be legally hired, always turning over any money she made to her mother.

One day on her way to work during her junior year of high school, a motorcyclist was killed when he slammed into the side of the car Erin was driving. Although she was not at fault, she was charged with involuntary manslaughter. Erin was horrified when a court-appointed attorney suggested that she plead guilty to the charge to lessen the likelihood of a long sentence. Her mother could not afford to hire an attorney to plead her daughter's case, so Erin talked her into mortgaging their home to make this possible. She was acquitted, which was good news, but as a sixteen-year-old girl, she had a lot to overcome.

Erin went on with her life, graduating from high school with honors. She started college, married her high school sweet-heart, and worked every

> "The greatest part of our happiness or misery depends upon our dispositions, and not upon our circumstances."
> —Martha Washington

spare minute, finally earning enough money to pay back her mother. Grand dreams of a better life never entered her mind. She was just happy to pay off her past and get it behind her.

One night about ten years later, she was feeling depressed and desperate. She was waiting for her baby to arrive and for her husband, Bob, an Air Force pilot who was out for days at a time on training missions, to come home. To help pass the time, Erin turned on the TV. Billy Graham was speaking. She listened as he talked about how God had made it possible for her to have a better life than she had experienced so far. To Erin, this sounded too good to be true, but she was unhappy, desperate, and ready to try anything. As she describes it, she "prayed to the TV" and asked God to take over her mess of a life. She called the toll-free number on the screen and requested Dr. Graham's free materials.

A book and some pamphlets arrived a few days later, and soon Erin was learning more about God's promises. She discovered that God invites us to pray and bring Him our requests regarding what we would like to see happen in our lives and the lives of others. This was a new idea to her—something she had never heard before. Based on God's offer, for the first time in her life she allowed herself to dream about what could be and prayed about those dreams.

Instead of her usual patterns of thinking—*This is just the way things are. . . . Everyone's got to play the cards they've been dealt, and mine aren't so good. . . . Happiness and success are for other people, not me*—she began to envision a better future and pray about what God might do. As promised, He started answering her prayers.

When Bob returned home from his trip, Erin told him about her new faith in God and asked him to read what she had been reading. He wasn't eager to comply but finally agreed to do so.

As a result he, too, decided to accept God's offer of a better and eternal life. They began growing in their faith and rebuilding their marriage.

One of Erin's first prayers was about her dream to finish her college degree. Although the Air Force required that they move frequently, she enrolled in college classes wherever possible. It took her eleven years at ten universities to earn enough credits, but she finally received a bachelor's degree in business.

Erin also dreamed of becoming a successful businesswoman, so she began praying about it. God began answering her prayers by opening doors for jobs wherever the military moved their family. Today, twenty-one years later, Erin is listed among the top ten female financial planners in the country and is a faithful follower of Jesus.

What about You?

Do you dream of a better life? Are you desperate for change? Do you believe that God cares about your desperation, the details of your life? that He wants to get personally involved in helping you manage your schedule, get your home in order, rebuild your marriage, parent your children, make wise decisions, face pain with courage, experience personal peace, and become your best self? According to the Bible, He does.

Matthew 10:30 says, "Even the very hairs of your head are all numbered." I love this verse because it tells me, a woman who loses enough hair daily to stuff a pillow, that God continually has to recount. I figure that if He cares about the hair caught in my hairbrush, He cares about broken appliances; crowded calendars; strong-willed children; empty pantries, gas tanks, and bank accounts; and every other problem we encounter. Actually, the Bible says that He cares about us more than we can imagine, loves us more than we can comprehend, and invites us to tell Him when we feel frustrated and need help.

God's Part and Our Part

God not only tells us to pray, He tells us to obey. There are things that only God can do for us and times when only His direct intervention will solve a problem. But God has also given us resources that He wants us to use faithfully as we call on Him for help. Among these resources are our minds, our abilities, and our relationships. He has also given us wisdom in His Word about how to live wisely.

When my friend Erin began to experience some relief from the financial hole her family was in, she didn't go out and spend everything. She was faithful to take advantage of opportunities for work and education that God opened up for her. Every time she got a raise, she chose to save 50 percent of the increase rather than step up their lifestyle. She chose to be content with less than she could afford, which not only put her family on a firm financial foundation, but it allowed them to have plenty to give away as well.

Waiting around for God to act on the things you can't do when He has given you some things you *can* do is a little like asking Him to lower your cholesterol while continuing to eat fat-laden foods. He expects us to live wisely and change the things we can while at the same time praying about the things we can't.

Faith is "the assurance of things hoped for, the conviction of things not seen" (Hebrews 11:1, NASB). It's about believing that things are true even when we can't see them. I encourage you to step out in faith and act as if what the Bible says about some area of concern is true. If you're praying that God will help you love your husband, step out and do something to serve him. Count on God's love to act through you whether you feel like it or not. But, you may ask, *Isn't that hypocrisy?* No, not if you are acting on what the Bible says. Actually, it's hypocritical to say you believe in the Bible and not obey what it says, even when you don't "feel like" it will make a difference. Emotions are a powerful part of our lives and can't be shoved aside, but they are not a good indicator of the truth either. They are like a thermometer that takes our internal emotional temperature, but they make a very poor thermostat. God's Word is a much more

> "If any of you lacks wisdom, he should ask God, who gives generously to all without finding fault, and it will be given to him."
> *(James 1:5)*

reliable thermostat, and we can change our emotional temperature by choosing to be obedient to His truth.

Bit by Bit

Arriving at the point of desperation doesn't just happen overnight. When we choose not to take control of our lives, we fall prey to destructive habits, poor decisions, and a less-than-satisfying life. When we put off making changes, little problems can easily grow into big ones. A problem Bill and I encountered in our first home serves to remind us of this principle.

We had a small leak in one of the water pipes connected to our washing machine. By the time we finally discovered it, the entire kitchen floor had rotted and had to be replaced. A relatively minor amount of water leaking over time had caused a big, expensive problem. If we had known it was happening, we would have done something immediately. But we could have decided, *Well, it's such a small amount of water; what can it hurt?* Unfortunately, this is often how we reason when making important decisions about our homes and families. Small problems left unattended can have big repercussions.

But it's also true that small positive changes can have big repercussions in a good sense. For example, creating a family rule that whenever you buy something new, something old goes out the door will help you keep clutter at bay. Deciding that every night your family will do some housecleaning for ten minutes (in that time you could vacuum a couple of rooms, fold a load of clothes, or wipe off mirrors and fixtures in the bathroom) will help you keep on top of housework. Committing to saying you're sorry to family members when unkind words slip out will help you be mindful of changing the way you communicate and set a good example for your kids.

A Deeper Kind of Change

The Family Manager system and solutions will help you bring order to your home and balance to your life. But they only provide help up to a certain point. They cannot give you patience toward your children; help you forgive your husband when he hurts you; fill you with love for unlovable people; give you joy in the midst of painful circumstances; or make you a kinder, gentler, more contented person. Only God can do that.

> "Come near to God and he will come near to you."
> *(James 4:8)*

Only you can decide how desperate you are to experience this kind of change in your life, and it's only wrought by drawing near to God.

Desperate people find it easier to draw near to God—precisely because they are desperate. Far from being offended by our coming to Him, many times as a last resort, God welcomes us with open arms. Over the years I've learned at least three things about drawing and staying near to God.

1. Don't let guilt keep you from getting the help you need.

The guilt we naturally feel about messing up our lives is not meant to keep us from God but to drive us to Him. When we feel desperate, it's easier to put away pride and come anyway, unworthy as we may feel. So what if your life and your home is in bad shape? What if you've made a lot of mistakes you're ashamed of? Who hasn't? God loves to forgive when we come honestly to Him. Part of the misery we feel is God's gracious gift to remind us that we can't make life work without Him. Desperate people learn that guilt is the soul's cry for the love of God, and they draw near to Him to find the grace and mercy they need.

2. God's acquaintance isn't made by occasional visits. The older—and hopefully wiser—I get, the more desperate I get to know my Creator. When I was younger my life had a predictable pattern that I deeply regret. When things got bad, I ran to God's side. When things were good again, I wandered. I never want to fall into that trap again, because it causes me, and a lot of other people, pain. I get up every morning and spend time reading and studying God's Word—listening to Him—and praying—talking with Him. I want to be a wise person, so I spend a lot of time reading and thinking about Proverbs. I want to know God, so I read the Gospels, since Jesus defines God in human flesh.

3. Seek God together. If your husband or another family member is interested, by all means take time to read, pray, and draw near to God together. It's also helpful to draw near to

God with other like-minded women. We need each other for encouragement, support, understanding, rescue, and the opportunity to give away what we have learned.

If you count yourself amongst the millions of desperate households, that's not as bad as it may sound. You likely know things need to change, and you know you need help. God is ready and waiting when you are.

Acknowledgments

It takes a team to manage a family—and to write a book.

To my husband, Bill; our three boys, John, Joel, and James; and our daughter-in-law, Genevieve, I thank God for each of you. If our love for each other wasn't so unconditionally strong and our family wasn't as fun and supportive as it is, I wouldn't be writing this book or able to fulfill my calling to help other families experience what we have. I love you all.

To my trusted business partners and colleagues who care deeply about the cause of helping families and have invested time, money, ideas, and energy to bring about a national network of Family Manager Coaches. I sincerely thank David Waldrep, president of Family Manager Network; Larry Ragland and Chris Gaines at Isphere, our technology partners; Cynthia Pharr Lee of CPharr and Company, our public relations partners; Dan Johnson, longtime friend and president of the Idea Agency; and Patti Dematteo, also a longtime friend and president of Ultimate Performance. I love each of you and appreciate your dedication to this important endeavor.

To my publishing partners at Tyndale House Publishers, especially Jan Long Harris and Doug Knox. Thank you for believing in my vision for Picket Fence Press books and the cause of bringing fresh resources to soothe the hearts and meet the needs of busy, modern women. And to all of the Tyndale family members who have put in long hours to make this book happen on time—my editor, Kim Miller; Nancy Clausen, Sarah Atkinson, Erik Peterson, and Yolanda Sidney from marketing and production; and Sharon Leavitt—the glue that holds everything together—I offer my heartfelt appreciation.

To Family Manager Coaches and the families with whom you've worked, I appreciate your willingness to share your stories so that other families can be encouraged and reap rich rewards from the lessons you've learned and the challenges you've overcome. And to dear friends Judie Byrd, Pam Pfeffer, Peggy Zadina, and Erin Botsford, who offered their stories and expertise to the book, and to Ann Matturro and Tyra Banks for their excellent research and editing help.

To my faithful physicians and friends, Dr. Kathryn Waldrep, Dr. Rosemary McCoy, Dr. Alison Laidley, and Dr. Patrick Hodges, who have worked around my speaking and writing schedule to take me from an early-stage breast cancer diagnosis to the 100 percent cure category, I thank God for your skills and dedication.

About the Author

Kathy Peel is called "America's Family Manager" by journalists and millions of women. She is founder and CEO of Family Manager Network, Inc., a company that provides resources and Family Manager Makeover services through a national network of certified Family Manager Coaches.

She is AOL's Family and Kids' Coach and editor-at-large for Picket Fence Press, and she writes for many magazines.

Visit www.familymanager.com to sign up for Kathy's free newsletter, to learn about Family Manager coaching and makeovers, or to contact Kathy about speaking at an event.

Picket Fence Press

*An inspiring collection of journeys down the paths of life . . .
for those who dream of a happy, well-managed home,
a place where you and your family long to be,
an atmosphere where your children can flourish and relationships deepen.*

Come and join us . . .

*as we discover new places, purposes, and hope for a balanced life,
learning secrets from other busy women,
nurturing our souls while stretching our faith,
and finding fulfillment in the important work we do every day.*

Look for Picket Fence Press books, an imprint of Tyndale House Publishers,
everywhere books are sold.

A FAMILY MANAGER RESOURCE

Making home your favorite place to be

CP0174